Shiela

In Search of the Eider

Somateria mollissima sedentaria.

In Search of The Eider

Peter M Driver

Illustrations by David Bygott

The Saturn Press

Published by The Saturn Press Limited,
116a Pentonville Road, London N1 9JN

First published 1974

Set in 11/12pt. Baskerville by
Dahling Dahling, 331 Grays Inn Road,
London WC14 8PX
and printed by Compton Printing Limited,
Aylesbury and London

ISBN 0 904196 00 3

Contents

Introduction

This book is about the eider – the sea duck which provides down for bedding and ducklings for researchers such as myself. If the book is opened at random one might be surprised at finding oneself in the middle of a discourse about the nature of adolescence or the psychology of exploration. But there is some method in this apparent madness, for I have tried to give the background to my work with eider ducklings. Thus the biological background is given in chapter 1 and the geographical background in chapter 2. Then in chapter 3 I introduce the species properly for the first time, going on in chapter 4 to give a general account of the problems and rewards of playing the part of a female eider, rearing my own ducklings. The following chapters on hatching, infancy, and adolescence follow fairly naturally, though again, in the last chapter, one might be surprised to find oneself involved in a consideration of the relative success of eider and human or biological ponderings on the future of Man.

I feel that many scientists, or any other specialists for that matter, are too narrow in their outlook. In the academic field for example one finds that all too often people specialise to the extent that they spend their lives finding out more and more about less and less. As has been pointed out before, the logical conclusion of this is the elucidation of everything about nothing. This is obviously an exaggeration, yet it is disturbing to find how many well-qualified people have a very limited knowledge or understanding of things outside their own narrow field. True, with our rapidly increasing knowledge, specialists have to spend increasing amounts of time getting to grips with their subject. And in science at least, one has to isolate discrete phenomena for purposes of study. But it is not necessary to keep the blinkers on when the study is complete. With life increasing in complexity at an accelerating rate I think it is important that more people should try to integrate different aspects of our culture and try to communicate their understanding to others. This is why I have spread myself widely in this book. Such an approach is of course fraught with dangers of misunderstanding and misinterpretation – to say nothing of the logistic problems of earning one's living from integrational activities – but I hope the result as presented here will be found to be worthwhile.

As the events described in this book are not presented in chronological order, I should explain that it is all built around two expeditions which I made into the Canadian arctic during the summers of 1958 and 1959 when I was a graduate student in Zoology at McGill University, Montreal. On both expeditions I had the invaluable assistance of Clive W. Nicol who came from his school in England – where I had taught him and we had become friends – to be my virtual slave. In the first summer we went into Ungava in Quebec-Labrador, making camp on False River at the southern end of Ungava Bay. In our second summer we were more adventurous and proceeded, with some difficulty, to the Belcher Islands in Hudson Bay where we camped at the mouth of Kasegalik River on Flaherty Island.

Of course, expeditions of the kind I describe do not just happen; they have to be engineered, and the processes of that engineering can often be very complex. The basic requirement is for people with an exploratory drive high enough to overcome the problems attendant upon actually getting into the field. Many people would like to explore in out-of-the-way places, but such explorations have to be financed and, except for the rare exception of the rich dilettante, monies have to be competed for. Such monies are available in restricted amounts for a few exploration societies, research institutions, and universities. In my case I was fortunate in that the scholarship I obtained actually required me to carry out research in the arctic. I could have studied eiders in Britain but money was not there available – or, perhaps, I hadn't found how to get at it – and so I had the double advantage of getting support for exploration and for work on my chosen animal.

So far so good. But having obtained one's support, there remains the problem of implementing one's plans. In this respect I cannot speak too highly of Clive Nicol – or 'Nic', as he is known to friends and colleagues. I most certainly could not have made a success of my work without his special kind of support. Still a teenager fresh from school, he came through a very difficult two seasons' work with great merit. Our relationship was a symbiotic one; as in other examples of extreme symbiosis in the organic world we were, in our special situation, dependant on each other. My grant provided the money for the expeditions – including Nic.

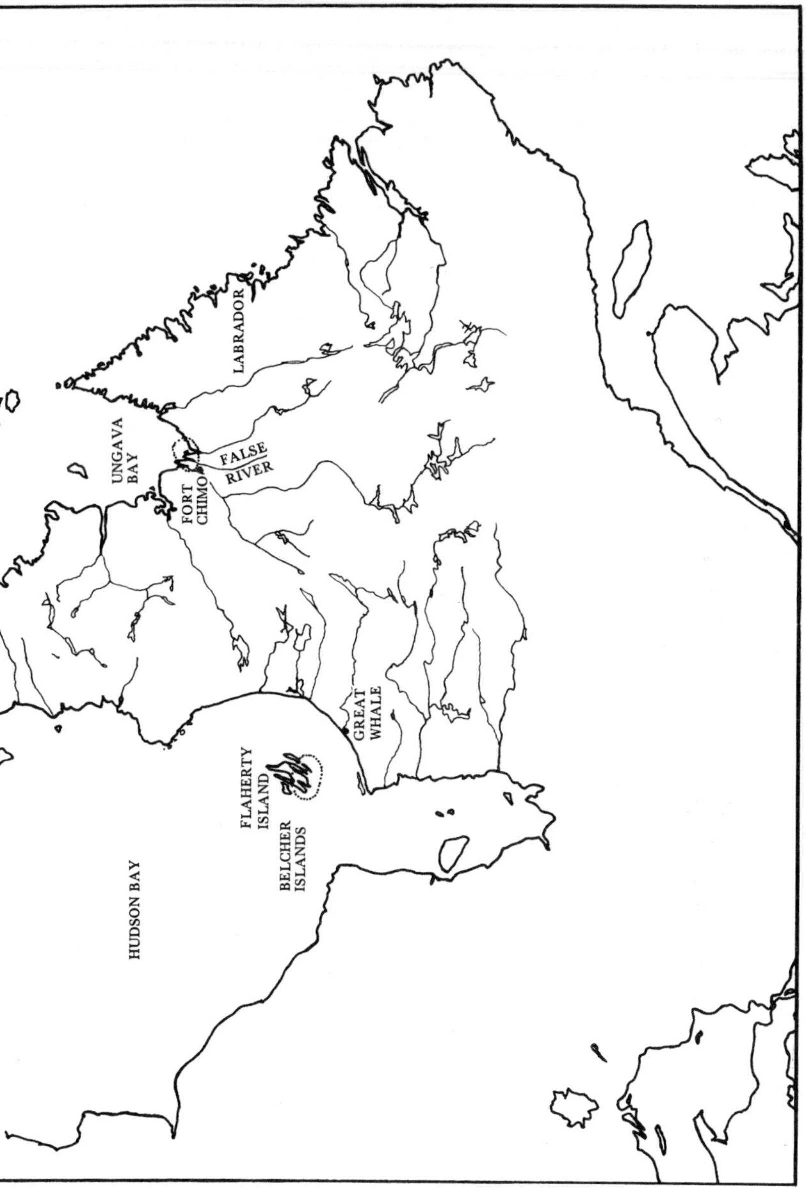

Eastern Canada showing study areas

His support made it possible for me to carry out the procedures. It could be said that many young males would leap at the opportunity to go into the north on such a venture as mine, and indeed that is so. But there are few with the required qualities of inquisitiveness, determination, and self-discipline — to say nothing of physical fitness and courage — that are necessary in a field assistant for out-of-the-way places. And in my case the requirements were even more rigorous. I had little money to spend on food or drink and my equipment was somewhat spartan, so my assistant had to expect a certain amount of hardship. Additionally, I tend to stretch myself to the limit and undertake more projects and tasks than I really should and my poor assistant has to fit into the same pattern, helping with a wide and trying spectrum of activities. I made it clear to Nic that after an appropriate apprenticeship period I expected him to be able to perform his allotted tasks as efficiently as I would myself. A little severe perhaps, and maybe big-headed on my part, but he lived up to this admonition. It was a minor hell at the time, but Nic has appreciated his apprenticeship since. He subsequently was on a major arctic expedition and had a rather poor opinion of the standards of many of the other personnel, having been set such high standards on our two trips.

I think I should point out that Nic was of great physical strength. Not very tall and with childhood memories of bullying, among other things, he had, by the time he was 18, built himself up by exercise, judo, and jujutsu, into a formidable fighting machine. I think one of the reasons he had a kind of respect for me was the fact that I was just about the only person who wasn't afraid of him. He had introduced me to judo also, and I was a little faster and quicker with my reflexes than he was. But I wouldn't dream of tangling with him now. He later got a black belt — the hard way, in Tokyo.

Nic's physical powers were of great value in our work. When, as I explain later, we had to build a hut, Nic was able to carry huge poles from the tree line, and roll up enormous boulders. I was fairly fit myself at the time and didn't think anything of it, but looking back upon it all the amount of physical as well as mental work we got through was enormous. Sometimes however, Nic's powers were a mixed blessing. In our second summer for example, when we arrived in the northern settlement which was to be the take-off point for our final destination, an Eskimo dog was causing trouble and had actually killed a native child. The authorities seemed to have a laissez-faire attitude to the situation —

apparently because it was not a white child who had been killed. The dog still roamed the camp – as happens all too often when dog teams are not being used – and we were furious. Particularly Nic. That same evening, after he had been rather quiet for some time, he got up and put on his outdoor things – including gloves which he seldom wore – and prepared to go out into the sub-arctic night. He was obviously going after the dog. I knew I wouldn't be able to dissuade him and so just cautioned him to be careful. He didn't find it, which was probably just as well. A couple of days later however he found something more interesting: a human skeleton, partly exposed in the river bank. A white man, almost entirely decomposed. With a bruised skull. And marks of burning. I put it in the camp fridge. But that is all another story.

Nic was also extremely tenacious. This was occasionally a disadvantage when combined with his feeling of physical power – as on the occasion he was blown away in a gale, recounted later. But usually it was very helpful. For example, when I lost the sweep hand off my stop watch on the littered floor of our lab tent he scoured that floor 'til he found it, finally having to sweep up all the bits and burn off the organic debris, leaving behind the precious bit of metal.

Another qualification my assistant had to have was a distinct sense of humour, and in this I knew that Nic was well-equipped. While still at school – he as pupil and me as teacher – we had developed an unusual type of collaboration in the production of nonsense stories and verse. So I knew we were likely to get on together – a very important factor when one is likely to be isolated in the middle of nowhere for months on end with no one else to talk to.

So our association really was a symbiotic one, each providing something essential for the well-being of the other in the circumstance in which we found ourselves. Indeed, it is generally recognised now that psychological as well as other factors are of great importance in the choosing of expedition personnel, and an expedition may stand or fall on the degree of matching of temperaments of its members.

Nic was also able to take a weight off my shoulders in the lengthy preparation period before we went north, both in Britain and in Canada. There are so many things to do, from the making of special crates for the equipment (after it has been begged, borrowed, or even bought) to the working out of schedules for the transport of that equipment by rail, air and boat, that one man with a full-time job doing other things would be hard-pressed to get through it all. And in many ways the preparations for an expedition are as important to the outcome as the conduct of the expedition proper.

1 Ethology and Exploration

I think I should start by explaining what ethology is – or at least what *I* consider it to be. It is animal behaviour looked at from the point of view of the scientific naturalist. Konrad Lorenz has called ethology the "biology of behaviour", and this is a very good definition, but it is not self-explanatory. Biology is the scientific study of life; of all living organisms, including man. It is concerned with the wonderful, complex, many-faceted nature of organisms and their evolution. While it is the most difficult of all subjects to understand in its entirety, biology also has the greatest rewards: of intellectual stimulation and challenge, of excitement in the unravelling of its complexities, of satisfaction in the uncovering of some previously hidden fact of life, and of aesthetic enrichment. For the science of life can quite properly be brought to bear upon any problem of existence, any organism from microbe to Man, and any living process from the chemical changes inside single cells to the dynamic interactions between whole communities. It can help to explain life and death, peace and war, beauty and ugliness, truth and falsehood. Any living process can come under its scrutiny, even though we are only just beginning to understand the biology of just a few of those processes.

Biology can be studied at many levels of organisation. One can 'biologise' upon the whole individual organism, which is what most ethologists and ecologists try to do. Or one can study the organism's constituent parts – its organs, or the tissues of which they are composed, or, in turn, the cells which make up those tissues. Or one may study the 'super-organism' – the community which is the result of the mutualistic interactions of a number of organisms. These may be the total community of individuals in a single species, or the community of several species existing in the same habitat. Ethologists and ecologists have interests at the community level also, the ethologists studying the interactions between the animals, and ecologists those between the animals and their environment. This is an over-simplification of course, but I think it gives a fair picture of the situation as a whole.

Also, we should remember that the ethologist, no less than the anatomist or the environmental ecologist, is studying just one representative section of an ongoing evolutionary process: the animal's *present* relationship with others. This fact is often forgotten, or ignored, even by ethologists. As evolution by natural selection is part of the central philosophy of all biology, any study of the living organism should, ideally, take into account that organism's past history. As T. H. Huxley put it "a fossil animal differs only in this regard from a stuffed one, that the one has been dead longer than the other, for ages instead of for days."

Behaviour of course does not fossilise, but we can deduce a great deal from the structure of fossils as to the nature of their behaviour for, if we compare the behaviour of living animals, we can see – if we study them well enough – that such-and-such a structure is used in this or that way, whereas another structure will be used quite differently. And we can build up a general picture of the behaviour of a living species, and compare it with the behaviour of another. So, just as a good 'bone man' will be able to look at a fossil bone and say not only what bone it is but also what sort of animal it came from, so will a good behavioural biologist be able to make a guess at how that animal moved. And if he knows what the environment of his fossil was like he will have a good idea of how it lived. Then, by comparison with living forms, he will be able to build up a sort of fossil behaviour for that animal-that-was. I say this largely to stress the fact that behaviour, no less that physical structure, has evolved from pre-existing, usually simpler forms.

Ethology then, is the study of the animal's behavioural inter-relationship with the other animals in its environment – both of its own species and of others with which it comes into conflict or competition. This means that ethology, ideally, is based upon field studies. To understand an animal's behaviour as an evolved, and evolving complex of give and take between itself and other animals in its natural environment one should begin by going into that environment and seeing for oneself what goes on. As a result, field ethologists are still regarded by some other kinds of scientists as an over-cute breed of nature boys specialising in anecdote, but this is far from the truth. Not every ethologist goes to the extreme environmental lengths that I describe in this book to get to grips with his study material, but, however much experimental and analytical work is done in the laboratory with animals, the results are relatively meaningless if one does not know the natural behaviour of the species first. Some extremely impressive work is carried out by laboratory ethologists, and by their scientific cousins the comparative psychologists, but the field work should come first.

Of course, for those of us who are predisposed to working out of doors the field ethologist's life can seem to be a very enviable one. I remember, many years ago now – when I was an assistant at the Wildfowl Trust, with an honours zoology degree freshly tacked onto my name – sitting in the sunshine with the world's leading ethologist, Konrad Lorenz. I was secretly in transports of delight – to be sitting with the great Lorenz, whose *King Solomon's Ring* was just coming out in English – but I was also concentrating very hard on the biological spectacle laid out before us. We were watching ducks. They were displaying very nicely, posturing, grunting, whistling, and splashing in their rituals of pair-formation. Lorenz could understand what was going on better than anyone alive, and I was going to make full use of my opportunity. Occasionally he would make a remark, or I would venture a question, but for the most part we were silent. For an hour or more we sat there trying, as Lorenz himself put it, to "get inside the skins" of those animals: to so concentrate on what they were doing that one could almost feel for oneself what it was like to be one of them. This concentration must have given us the appearance of somnolents, and after a while Lorenz quietly said "You know – anyone watching us would think we were just enjoying the sunshine – but really we're working very hard!" We were. But we were also appreciative of the solar bonus.

But one must remember that the sun does not always shine. I have been more cold, wet, hungry, miserable, and frightened at various times during my ethological field studies than at any other times in my life – except for a few occasions in (or thrown out of) small boats off the wild Welsh coast. The field ethologist is frequently frustrated in his efforts to observe a particular piece of behaviour – even, sometimes, in his efforts to find his study animal! But somehow it is all worth it. There are few things as exciting, humbling, and awe-inspiring, all in one, as the partial unfolding of a small part of nature's complexity after long hours, or years, of study. One has difficulty, of course, in getting sufficient funds to support one's work. So, very often it is partially financed out of one's own, or one's family's pocket. One never has enough equipment of the right sort in the right place at the right time, or enough assistance in the field or back in the lab working out one's results. But at least, one feels that one's results are meaningful in a special sort of way: if the work has been done properly the results form part of the reflection of truth in the mirror one is holding up before nature. And if one holds the mirror correctly, the reflection may be worth looking at. The field naturalist, after all, has the whole of living nature in his lap. The problem is what to do with it.

So the field ethologist tries to study, in as organised and disciplined a way as possible, the behaviour of animals in their natural environment. This kind of work became scientific when the behavioural wind of change began to blow across biology in the early 1930s. In Austria and Holland respectively Konrad Lorenz and Niko Tinbergen were studying animal behaviour in a truly scientific manner, Lorenz preferring to work with animals in semi-captivity and Tinbergen in the field. Between them they have contributed more to the development of ethology as a science than all other living biologists put together.

It has been my privilege to begin my ethological career with Lorenz when he first visited the Wildfowl Trust so many years ago, and much more recently to serve for a brief time as Tinbergen's Senior Research Officer at Oxford. As I have also worked in University zoology and psychology laboratories in England, Canada, and the U.S.A., as well as being a schoolmaster for 10 years, I think I understand a little about the disciplines and practitioners of ethology and psychology. Historically, the ethological viewpoint comes from biology; the psychological viewpoint from medicine. But more of that later.

The study of animal behaviour – in whatever way it is manifested – is just one of the many aspects of man's inquisitiveness; of his highly-developed drive to explore. All animals have this drive but in man it is more highly developed than any other species. And man is the only animal that can, to any meaningful degree, think. He is the only organism that can kick ideas around in its head. So man's exploratory drive shows itself not only in many kinds of exploration of the external environment by geographers and geologists, zoologists and botanists, navigators, explorers and adventurers, and others, it is also seen in the internal explorations of the great thinkers, whether they be artists or scientists, theoretical or practical, physical or metaphysical. In field ethologists and ecologists are combined both facets of exploration – external and internal. The field ethologist explores animal behaviour in the raw, in the field, in the wild, but he also explores its hidden meanings by trying new organisations of ideas inside his head. For this reason, if no other, his exploratory findings are likely to be more meaningful than those derived from manipulations of animals in artificial laboratory conditions.

We have only been thinking about life, to any real purpose, for about a century. Lorenz, Tinbergen, all eminent biologists owe their thinking, their discipline, their science, primarily to the great leap forward made collectively by the great nineteenth century natural scientists headed by Darwin, Wallace, and T. H. Huxley. With the publication in 1859 of Darwin's *The Origin of Species by Natural Selection* mankind entered a new era of potential for the understanding of himself and the world about him. And we have scarcely begun to make use of that potential. The study of animal – including human – behaviour is only just beginning to make sense, in spite of the millions in currency and man-hours that have been spent on it. We are only now – as a community – beginning to see that our relationship with our environment is important. Yet this is something which every successful organism has built in to its nature as a fundamental of existence: the mutualistic balance with the environment – including other organisms. We are only now beginning to realise, as a population, that our behaviour, like our structure, has evolved from that of simpler animals that have preceded us in evolutionary time. The success of *The Naked Ape* by ethologist Desmond Morris was, in part at least, due to the natural interest that the average thinking person now has in the animal origins of his behaviour. Sex is only one – though admittedly important – aspect of this.

But there has been a considerable dichotomy between the ethological and psychological approaches to the study of behaviour which, like the biassed extremes in the unnecessary schism between "The Two Cultures", has delayed the development of both. The two behavioural disciplines are at last drawing together, each beginning to see the advantages of the other's expertise, but there is still a long way to go. The reasons for this dichotomy, and delay, can be sought in the history of science. As a science, biology stood almost still from the time of Aristotle to Charles Darwin: over two thousand years. During that period the physical sciences developed at an impressive rate, being only occasionally hindered by the dogmas of established religion. In the study of living things, on the other hand, only medicine made any real progress, and that was of a limited nature.

Much of the responsibility for the delay in the development of biology as a science must be laid at the door of religious dogma. The central theme of biology – the theory of organic evolution, with its concomitant of adaptive change – was so inimical to the

tenets of theology that both time and the combined genius and courage of Darwin, Wallace, and Huxley were necessary for its gestation and birth. The physical sciences, including mathematics, on the other hand, in the absence of serious theological prohibition, were able to develop quite high standards of quality. Thus, when the theory of organic evolution came to be clearly stated, science was already largely built around mathematical concepts. Psychology developed from medicine as an anthropocentric science and, particularly in this century, has made increasing use of mathematical techniques in investigation and analysis. Comparative psychology – the branch of psychology which studies sub-human animals – lays particular emphasis upon experimental techniques in the laboratory and sophisticated statistical analysis of results and, by and large, is comparative only in so far as it compares the experimental performance of a relatively small number of easily domesticated animals such as the rat and the pigeon. It is not based upon biological modes of thought.

Ethology on the other hand, although still in its infancy and having yet to develop its own high standards of quality and definition, is based upon sound biological principles of evolution and adaptation. Of course there are different camps and schools of thought within ethology, and the two extremes are quite wide apart – as indicated by David's drawings of me in both roles. Some ethologists work entirely in the laboratory and wouldn't know what to do with an animal in the field if they saw one. Others go off into the wild blue yonder and are only seen every few years when they reappear to stock up with money, tobacco,

and spare socks. But on the whole, ethologists seem to have their feet on the ground – and as it is the ground outside, where the animals live too, these ethologists, if they are any good, learn an awful lot about animals.

The field ethologist, ideally, is a man of many parts. He should, of course, have a sound training in zoology, in addition to being an experienced field naturalist. The zoological training can be managed in about 5 years – say, 2 years in school VIth form and 3 years at University – but to acquire real expertise as a field naturalist takes a good deal longer. Fortunately, this latter qualification can be begun at a very early age and some of us, if we are lucky in our genes, or parental guidance, or environment – preferably all three – start before we are five years old. An interest in natural history is, after all, only a civilised modification of the ancient urge to explore our environment and hunt animals, and it is natural for this interest to appear early in life. The experienced field naturalist thus develops the faculties of the hunter – senses highly attuned to pick up information from the environment; the ability to move through that environment with the minimum of noise and disturbance; and the ability to blend, motionless, into the background, and thus see without being seen. It is remarkable the degree to which one can develop one's senses through experience and practice – though it is probably the brain that is becoming more efficient rather than the sense organs themselves. One's visual information system thus becomes many times more efficient than the average city-dweller's, not only recording a great deal of information from both near and far, but also developing the ability to register information from the periphery of the visual field with the result that if anything interesting occurs to one side of one's line of focused sight one's attention can be brought to bear upon it. Similarly with the auditory information system. One learns to take in auditory information from all around all the time, and if one has learned, by experience, the sounds of nature, one is constantly surrounded by a spectrum of meaningful sounds – the squeaking of shrews in the grass, the rustle of mice or voles in the leaves, the scratching of a wasp's jaws as it chews particles of wood off a post to make its paper nest, or the cracking of seeds as finches feed in the trees. Even the sense of smell can be developed to a degree which most people would find remarkable. The scents of fox and most domestic animals are easy to distinguish, but one can also tell, by the sense of smell, whether an empty tree hole is regularly visited by jackdaw or owl, or if a cliff-top burrow belongs to a rabbit or a shearwater. And when the senses are used in combination, as they usually are, one's walk through the countryside can be almost overwhelmingly full of information.

The good field naturalist is also highly adaptable – something which is made clear, I trust, in the next chapter, where I consider the occasional necessity for major adaptations to environmental pressures. But adaptation in little things is important too, and here I cannot resist a couple of very similar anecdotes. Once, in Charles Darwin's early beetle-collecting days, he had captured two interesting specimens, one in each hand, when he saw another, even more interesting. So he popped one of his captures into his mouth. But he got more than he had bargained for, because the one in his mouth exuded an extremely bitter secretion as a defence mechanism, was ejected, and escaped. Something basically similar happened to me some years ago when I was instructing a party of students in the art of observation and collection of animals of the sea shore. I too had a specimen in each hand when I saw another I particularly wanted. I too popped one specimen – a small blenny (a common shore-living fish) – into my mouth. I knew that blennies weren't bitter, but this was a case of the biter bit, because that little fish took a mouthful of the lining of my cheek and hung on. I had to stand with my mouth foolishly open until it let go. On these two occasions of course the human adaptation was not very successful. But, on the whole, particularly if one knows the potential defences of one's animal, the mouth is a perfectly satisfactory temporary receptacle while one's hands are being emptied.

The adaptations I am referring to are the short-term adaptations made possible by man's ability to think. In these the naturalist usually has the advantage over his study material. But when it comes to the long-term adaptations that organisms have evolved and perfected over thousands or millions of generations, then the naturalist, however skilled, is often beaten. A favoured anecdote illustrating this concerns two of the great American naturalists, William Beebe and William Morton Wheeler, when they were collecting in the jungles of British Guiana. Wheeler was exhorting his companion to be very careful in accepting reports of the effectiveness of insect mimicry without complete evidence. He then picked up a fresh specimen, only to throw it down again immediately. On close inspection he found that what appeared to be a wasp that had tried to sting him was in fact a moth with the shape, colour, and even the 'stinging' movements of a wasp. "Beebe" Wheeler went on – "believe anything you damned well please about mimicry."

A comparable story concerns an occasion when I was collecting on the Devonshire sea shore with my friend Middy, who will appear again later in the book. A fish I had disturbed from under a large rock had darted away and taken refuge under a smaller rock. But I had seen where it went and approached the rock cautiously and began to feel carefully beneath it with both hands – one can often capture fish with the bare hands in this way, if sufficiently experienced. But Middy suddenly said, urgently, "Stop. Don't move!" and approaching cautiously pointed out that the 'rock' beneath which I was feeling was in fact a particularly fine specimen of the scorpion fish, a species whose structural camouflage is matched by its immobility when disturbed. Its similarity to an alga-encrusted stone was so great that it had fooled both the smaller fish and me.

The field naturalist, particularly if he is exploring in out-of-the-way places, often has to combine adaptability with a good deal of patience and physical endurance. A fair illustration of this, I think, is the story of our second journey into the northland in our second summer of duckling study. We had decided, after our first summer in Quebec-Labrador – with its attendant difficulties which I explain in the next chapter – to go for somewhere even more isolated but where we might be able to find Eskimo help in our search for eider nests. I settled for the Belcher Islands in Hudson Bay, discovered for the white man not many decades before and explored by the great film-maker Robert Flaherty. These islands are just a speck on the map of North America but they cover about 70 square miles of the great inlet of the arctic ocean which is Hudson Bay, are very much dissected by bays, inlets, creeks, lakes and rivers, and form splendid breeding grounds for a variety of waterfowl. When eventually we established camp there our nights were enlivened by the weird calls of the common loon (great northern diver), and various species of ducks and other water-fowl were seldom out of view or earshot. But the adventures of actually getting to our chosen camp site are what I want to discuss at the moment, and the birds must wait until later.

On the coast of Hudson Bay a mere 70 miles to the south east of the Belchers lies the settlement of Great Whale – on the estuary of the river of that name – supplied by a commercial air line. So at the time of 'break-up', when the rivers unfreeze and the snow is beginning to melt, Nic, my faithful assistant ('temporary slave' might be a better term) flew up with our equipment and stores and I followed as soon as my University duties allowed. From experience of the previous summer's difficulties we knew we had to be settled in our chosen base camp site as soon as possible after the break-up. Fortunately there was a very experienced northern bush-pilot with his own sea plane at Great Whale – a twin-engined 'Canso', which we knew as the 'Catalina' during the war – who agreed to try to get us to our chosen destination, which was the estuary of Kasegalik River where it flowed into Robertson Bay on Flaherty Island – the biggest of the Belcher group.

But our first major problem faced us immediately: we had too much gear for the plane's supposed capacity. Mindful of food problems the season before, we had taken enough to be self-sufficient if we could not live off the land, and our tentage was bulkier too – again as a result of experiences which are recounted later in the book. And we had a small dory and outboard motor in addition to our kayak so that we could move loads by water if necessary. Bob, the big, burly cigar-smoking bush pilot worked out his payload figures again and again, only to conclude that we simply had too much to carry. But I didn't have enough money to charter the plane for two trips, and after much cajoling and obvious near-despair on our side he agreed to try. "But" he said "I can't guarantee to get off the water. If we do, I can't be sure we'll get there. And if we do get there I can't promise to put you down where you want to be." And of course I would have to pay him for the trip even if we had to return, unsuccessful. But it was a case of all or nothing.

Fortunately, two colleagues from the Fisheries Research Board had already decided on the same general area and Bob flew them out to Kasegalik Lake about 5 miles from where we wanted to be, and they were able to take some of our gear with them. But we were still heavily overloaded. And finally we found that our boat wouldn't go in the plane. It didn't take to pieces like the Fisheries canoes, and try as we would, we couldn't manoeuvre it through the plane's main hatch. So we had to tie it under one wing.

Overloaded, and unbalanced, the plane thundered over the water for what seemed to be miles but was, I suppose, only about half a mile, before we were airborne. Hudson Bay beneath us was a blinding glare of water and drifting ice floes as we approached the Belchers – a beautiful sight. But I wasn't able to appreciate the view to the full because the ropes tying our boat to the wing were coming loose and the dory was bobbling up and down in an ominous manner. I had visions of it dropping off and leaving us to move a ton or more of gear on foot, or with just the kayak. But we arrived over the Belchers, found the place where we wanted to be – and turned away again immediately. "Not a hope" said Bob "– rocks and ice floes". And so there were. Not nearly enough room to 'land' the plane in the estuary. So we just had to settle for the lake with our fisheries friends, and Bob did his run in towards it. Then, as we sped over the water at a few hundred feet, he suddenly put the nose of the plane down and dropped headlong at a steep angle in what seemed to me to be a most unusual manoeuvre. I went forward and leaned over his shoulder. "What are you doing?" I said. "There's rocks in this" Bob replied round his cigar " – I like to see where I'm goin'!" Then flattening out again he brought the plane down onto the water. We bounced quite a bit in a lumbering sort of way as the heavily loaded plane lost speed, and I had been amused by Bob's command to his young co-pilot (at least I think he was – he might just have been a friend, along for the ride) "switch on wipers!" as the spray burst heavily up over the front of the plane. But we came to a stop eventually and I shouted something to Bob about it being quite a smooth touch-down. "You kiddin'?" he said "Look outside!" I did. There was a three or four foot swell and we were drifting steadily towards the beach. Bob put his wheels down, as well as his floats, so that we couldn't ground in the shallows, and our friends came out with their canoe to help us unload. Which was just as well, because it would not have been too easy to get the boat from the wing, even though the ropes were loose. We unloaded and ferried everything to the shore and watched as Bob turned back into the wind to take off. He had quite a job to get the plane round as the wind was much stronger than we had realised, and he had to swing round in one direction and then as hard as he could in the other direction with the extra impetus, rather like the way one rocks a car out of a hole. Then he was away – the plane noticeably higher in the water! – and we were left in the middle of nowhere, with the wind rising.

Fortunately we were at the right end of the lake – it was nearly 40 miles long – and only had to cross the five miles or so to the other side where the river ran down to the estuary we were aiming for. But the wind went on rising and we had to stay put for a few days. Then when the water was safe for our rather small boats we ferried our stuff across to the other side where the water ran out to the sea. It took us all day and the mosquitoes in the evening were pretty bad, and we were tired, cross and uncomfortable. But, of course, there was much worse in store for us. We were five miles from the river mouth as the eider flies. It took us three days to get there. The river wound around and about like a demented serpent, with numerous rapids and shoals, few of them very dangerous but necessitating the unloading of the boats. They were then ridden down lightly and safely, while the gear had to be carried round the rough water. There were five of these "portages" to be negotiated, each involving several trips back and forth with heavy loads. The

Shooting rapids on way to camp on Belcher Islands

back-packing wasn't too bad, but we had vocabulary-testing trouble with our big drum of kerosene which David has illustrated for me in his inimitable style. It was too big to carry, and the ground was too uneven and waterlogged in patches for it to be rolled. And then I got a ducking unloading it from the big canoe at the head of a nasty stretch of rapids. But it floated. Of course! We could float it down. So we pushed it off into the main stream and went on with our portaging with lighter hearts and load.

But our relief was premature. We negotiated the next stretch of the river, and the next portage; and then the next; by which time the river was becoming shallower, slower and more broken by rocks and shoals. Our oil drum should have been in sight again now. But we couldn't find it. A scout on ahead didn't bring it to light, and I began to get really worried. That drum contained all our fuel for lighting, cooking, and the portable incubator Middy had designed and made for me. Its loss would be serious. So our friends went on ahead while Nic walked back upstream to try to find the errant article. I feared it was a forlorn hope, for the terrain was very much dissected by creeks and backwaters from the main river, and the largely-submerged oil drum might take days to find, if indeed we could find it at all. But Nic is nothing if

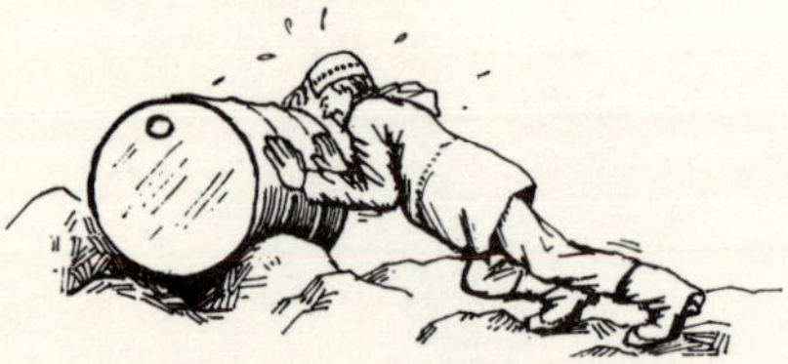

not tenacious, and after a few hours he found it, resting quietly in a backwater. From then on we kept a closer watch on it, and slowed our journey accordingly. We were near our destination anyway.

There was more trouble to come, however, before we could reach the mouth of the river and settle into our routine for the summer. The final portage was around a very shallow, shoally stretch of water, down which we had to paddle the dory without benefit of the outboard motor because of the danger of the prop' fouling a rock in the shallow water. Nic took the bow and I the stern, each with a paddle to try to guide the rather clumsy boat down the main stream. Not really a dangerous task, but tricky, because a side wind got up and the broad-beamed boat became almost impossible to steer in the slowly-moving waters. Things got more and more difficult as we narrowly missed a succession of small rocks and then the current and wind were taking us at increasing speed towards a bigger rock which, try as we would, we couldn't steer away from. I was shouting at Nic and he was shouting back at me as we swept down upon this monster about to take our dory away from us, but we simply couldn't steer away from it. And then came one of those split-second decisions out of nowhere which have saved so many dangerous situations. As we were about to crash into the rock I jumped sideways out of the dory into the water, using the impetus of my sideways movement to push the boat around the rock. Missing it by an inch or so, the boat went careering on down the river, Nic cursing even more because he was unaware of my sudden departure and being even less able to keep the boat from yawing back and forth. Puzzled, presumably by my silence, he looked back to see me crawling dripping out of the river. The water was quite shallow and I only went in up to my middle, and eventually was able to quietly share the joke with Nic, though he was almost convulsed as he brought the boat in to shore to collect me. The next morning we set up camp at the mouth of the river, nearly a week after landing on the lake 15 minutes eider-flight away.

That wâs a momentous summer for Nic and me. We had already been cut down to size by our previous tundra summer, but were now more experienced. We ate well – Nic had become a fine cook – though a visiting party of American geologists spurned our seal liver, roast duck, and arctic char. They preferred to eat out of tins. I got enough scientific material to complete my doctoral thesis. And Nic even managed to take a few minutes now and then to practice his jujutsu. He had set up a practice post on the beach camp site and would pound it energetically, much to the annoyance of our tame buzzard whose perch it was. The local Eskimos were very self-sufficient and very friendly, particularly their principal hunter, Noah, who became my close friend, and brought me the best of a brood of rough-legged buzzards they found on one of their forays. A somewhat macabre finishing touch to the picture was given by the fact that we had made the practice post in the form of a christian cross. I don't think we meant it disrespectfully. Perhaps it was bravado; perhaps ritual. I have never been quite sure.

For Nic the summer was also a serious one. Later in the season, when work was well under way and I had broods of ducklings "in full swing", Nic had a most unusual accident. We had a big cook tent with a fly-sheet over the top measuring about 12 by 12 feet square. One day the wind was so strong that the fly-sheet began to act as a sail and the metal tent poles began to bend. Nic couldn't

find me (I was in fact asleep in my tent after an arduous stretch of work) and decided he had to do something about the tent on his own. So, confident in his strength, he began to untie the fly-sheet guy ropes one at a time, hanging on to those already untied, but operating first *on the windward side.* Of course, when he got to the last rope the whole thing went up in the air with Nic on the end of it, and he was carried clean over the tent to land on the rocks on the other side. I found him later when the sound of the gale woke me up, unconscious amongst a litter of dried fish and eider skins. I carried him to his tent, after making sure his skull was not crushed, only concussed, and made him as comfortable as possible. We were several days journey from the nearest Hudson's Bay post where there might just possibly be some sort of medical aid or chance of communication with the outside world, but was it worth the move? I decided not, and I'm sure correctly so, for Nic came round, slowly, and was severely shaken, bruised, and concussed, but otherwise – apparently – unharmed. But that is only the beginning of the story, for later in the day, when I went in to his tent to check up he said "hey – I know why we're here and who you are and all that – but where did we come from? I can't remember anything else." And it was true. He had almost total amnesia with respect to his previous life. And it lasted until long after he got back to England at the end of our season's work. He didn't recognise anyone but his parents. During the summer a boat came in with mail, including one from Nic's girl friend. "I can't read this" he said, "I don't know the girl!" A somewhat tricky situation, the consequences of which make a story in themselves. But I just give the outline here to illustrate the problems that one has to be prepared for when working in out-of-the-way places. We were fortunate of course that our fisheries friends were close at hand, but it could well have been that we were on our own, and one has to be prepared for anything.

In the tundra, however, there are some things that one can only prepare for by experiencing them. The worst problem is the mosquitoes – as I explain in some detail in the next chapter. But another unexpected problem I had in Quebec-Labrador the previous summer was the disadvantage of only having two or three hours of semi-darkness per night and the dawn chorus consisting of the rather monotonous song of the white-crowned sparrow. The particular bird that had chosen our camp site as its territorial centre had an irritating habit of building its song up gradually – simple though it was – from the first tentative note or two,

through increasing numbers of syllables, until it actually achieved the full seven-note song. And it seemed to sing from my tent pole, it sounded so loud. It took me a long time to get used to that irritating bird; and then it gave up for the season. But I am proud to say that the only thing I threw at it was curses. But it was knowing what was coming every morning as the blasted bird 'tuned up' that was so annoying.

In the next chapter I tell more of our life in the tundra, and later unfold the story of my ethological studies with ducklings. But the ironic thing about it all is that it would have been a lot easier to do the whole thing in Britain! Not that I'm complaining: I had always wanted to work in the Arctic and when the opportunity came I was delighted to take it. But it all came about through the complexities of international economics. When I was at the Wildfowl Trust, research funds were almost unobtainable in Britain, and I had to leave and take up a post teaching biology – mostly VIth Form – at Cheltenham Grammar School. Nic was one of my pupils. Then, as I found myself successful in communicating biology to my students, and saw them go on to University, get their degrees, and then go on to do research, I became more and more frustrated. This was what I wanted to do myself – to study for a higher degree and get to grips with real research instead of just teaching the basics and reading about the work of others. So I looked round for the best research fellowship going, brashly applied for it – and got it! A Carnegie Arctic Research Fellowship tenable at McGill University in Montreal, with the summers to be spent in field work in the north. Marvellous! And so with my young family, including dog, squirrel, and several field mice, I set off across the Atlantic to begin the study which is the basis of this book. But if the money had been available in Britain I could have done the work just as well at home!

2 Life in the Tundra

The tundra lies around the brow of the world like a big fur muff around the Arctic Circle. But it is a muff in disarray for, with the tree line, it follows a wandering and intermittent course, straying north or receding south according to the terrain and, in large areas, interrupted by the waters of lakes or oceans. Text books and encyclopaedias tend to be rather coy and indefinite – and therefore misleading – in their descriptions of the tundra, partly, no doubt, because it is neither one thing nor the other: neither the full-blooded high arctic with ice and snow year-round and a very restricted fauna, nor the sub-arctic coniferous forest which every spring shakes off its snowy mantle and acts as host to a swarm of summer visitors as well as its hardy residents. But the tundra does have a character of its own, due to a particular mixture of geographical and biological features which give it a fascination equal in many ways to that of any other habitat.

"Tundra" is a Lapp word for the treeless grassland north of the coniferous forest, where the ground beneath the shallow surface layer of soil is permanently frozen, the winters are long and severe, and the average summer temperature is only around 10 degrees C (50° F). But although there is a short growing period of 60 to 90 days only, the summer tundra is covered with plant life, for there are many hours of daylight at that time, and in places the daytime temperature may reach 27 degrees C (80° F). The most numerous plants are grasses and sedges, with mosses and lichens – the principal food of the caribou or reindeer – and there are also some dwarf woody plants and several hardy species with bright flowers. These plants begin to show their seasonal growth before the snow thaws in early summer. Thus, with the melting of the snow the flowers appear, covering the ground with a magic carpet of rainbow dust that shimmers in the sun or gleams through the mist, while the snow still lies in large patches as if in some miraculous garden. Every summer the tundra re-creates thousands of square miles of ephemeral beauty.

There are vast tracts of tundra in both North America and

Wild flowers at False river in Labrador

Eurasia, and several species of animals, as well as plants, are common to both areas, for they were once united by the land bridge across the Bering Straits. But the short growing season and low average temperature limit the variety of animals that can flourish there. Most of the birds are migrants visiting the tundra for the short-lived but abundant and relatively untapped summer food supply. The only avian winter residents are the grouse or ptarmigan on land, a few species of ducks and auks at sea, and two predatory species – the rough-legged buzzard and the snowy owl. The raven also, in some areas, stays in the arctic all the year round.

The birds of prey, with their cousins who visit in the summer, and the mammalian predators such as fox, wolf, and weasel, depend largely for their well-being on the vast numbers of rodents that inhabit the tundra, albeit in greatly varying supply. The lemmings, and to a lesser extent the voles, are eaten in millions during the peak years of their unbalanced four-to-five-year breeding cycle. For centuries the lemmings have been demonstrating the perils of over-population, rollicking through their short lives with an almost human disregard for the consequences, feasting, to begin with, on the almost unlimited food supply, multiplying madly for a short time, and then succumbing to the

A rough legged buzzard, one of the arctic's predators

inevitable outcome of disease, starvation, universal strife, and – for the majority – death.

The predators are so dependent upon these rodents that when the prey population crashes every four years or so the predator populations follow suit. Our two tundra summers were crash years and we didn't see a single lemming or vole. Yet in peak years the rodents scatter from one's path like grasshoppers in a hayfield.

The tundra stretches north from the tree line to the high arctic where the snow never melts. But neither boundary is a clear-cut one. The tree line is not an obvious line around the northern hemisphere, like the abrupt division between a forestry plantation and the cultivated fields around. It is a belt which is sometimes several miles in breadth for, though the tundra is rather flat compared with other areas, there are many creeks and rivers and general undulations which are accompanied by trees and scrub in their wanderings through the wilderness. Thus, in the shelter of a creek boldly pushing northwards into the unknown one may find gnarled and adventurous spruce, larch, or willow trees above one's head, while a short step west or east, in flat open country, there is no tree in sight worthy of the name.

This southern transitional area where forest gradually gives way to tundra has been aptly named the *hemiarctic* for it is very much a half-and-half habitat. It is a kind of emulsion of trees and scrub in rough grassland. As one works northward the trees become fewer and fewer and the remaining vegetation hugs the ground to the horizon, the only possible response to the extremes of frost and wind. There is a good deal of water about, plenty of rock outcrop, and little soil. Drainage is generally poor and the summer soil is much waterlogged. But the ground cover of plants is rich and supports countless millions of individuals and hundreds of species of invertebrates, mostly insects and spiders, which in turn form the food of many of the species of birds and mammals.

The northern limit of the tundra also is a broad region of transition from one type of landscape to another; from summer sedges and flowers to year-round ice and snow. Here the bulk of species live in the sea, and the hardy peoples of the farthest north live almost entirely round the coastlines where they can reap the harvest of seals, sea birds and fish.

The transitional areas fringing the tundra have a transitional fauna, the forest species in the southern area pushing northwards in company with their vegetational requirements. Thus in Ungava we were camped in the hemiarctic belt where our bird neighbours came from both forest and tundra. There were American robins as well as white-crowned sparrows, blackpoll warblers as well as willow grouse. And in one sheltered spot I found a redpoll sitting on eggs in a spruce which was the last real tree in a straight line to the North Pole.

And the same with the water birds. During that summer we saw, in our small base area of just a few square miles, waterfowl of 12 different species belonging to 4 different tribes of ducks and geese. Those that bred in the area included green-winged teal and pintail, species typical of prairie, marsh or woodland pools, as well as eider, old-squaw, and red-breasted merganser, ducks to be expected in the tundra or on wild coastlines.

A pair of red-breasted mergansers

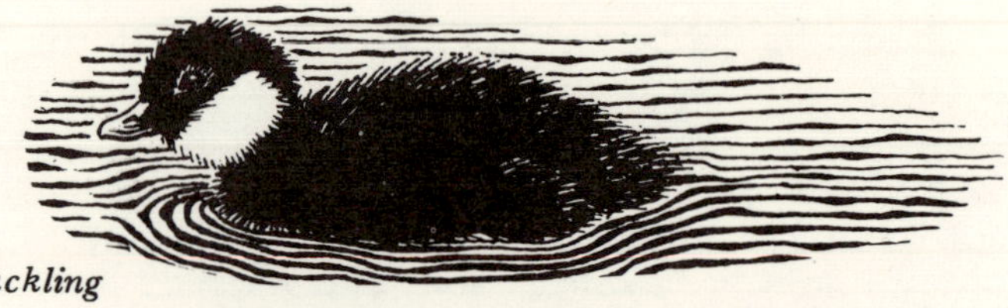

Old squaw duckling

Red-throated loon in flight

Red-necked phalarope

These northlands are something of a paradise for water birds, much of the arctic being water in some form or another. In the long winter it is largely locked up as ice and snow, but for two or three months there is an abundance of open water, both fresh and salt, in, around, and on the surface of which myriads of water birds can feed. Nearly 75 percent of arctic bird species are, in fact, birds of water or wetlands. In migration time, around the break-up, and then again before the freeze-up, the air is full of the sound of wings and the flock calls of waterfowl, waders, gulls, and loons, while the auks and terns come in from the open sea. The arctic tern in fact has come from the other end of the world, flying from the Arctic to the Antarctic and back again every year via the western coasts of Africa and Europe – a round trip of some 22,000 miles with, incidentally, summer at each end of the journey. There is, however, no equivalent to the tundra in the southern hemisphere, most of it being ocean, or antarctic ice, so only in the northlands do we see this immense seasonal fluctuation in numbers of water birds.

The major environmental problem facing all arctic animals is, of course, temperature regulation. Birds already have an excellent temperature control system which has enabled them to compete successfully with mammals. In particular, because it involved the development of feathers, it enabled them to fly, and this ability, which they have developed to an outstanding degree, means that, by migration, they are able to avoid the rigours of the arctic winter. Even so, the low average temperatures, the cold winds and, for the aquatic species, the particularly rapid loss of heat into the cold waters, combine to make temperature control a problem even in the tundra summer.

Various adaptations serve to cope with this problem. Large animals have a smaller surface area in proportion to their bulk than small animals, and hence they lose proportionately less heat. Arctic birds and mammals therefore tend to belong to species of large bulk. There are several adaptations for conserving heat, a well-known one being the development of layers of fat or blubber as insulation. Another insulating mechanism is seen in the feathered legs and feet of ptarmigan and snowy owls. And most people are aware of the particularly high insulating properties of the underdown of eider ducks – a feature shared with the other sea ducks, including old-squaw, harlequin, the goldeneyes, the mergansers and the scoters. All aquatic birds in fact have a particularly efficient insulating layer of down, the arctic species simply increasing this efficiency.

An interesting physiological mechanism for reducing heat loss is the system of vascular shunts, or counter-current system of blood flow, which is found in the legs of many species of birds and mammals which live in the arctic and other cold environments. In these species the arteries, taking blood to the limb extremities, pass close to the veins which collect the blood from those regions. This being so, the warm arterial blood loses much of its heat to the cool venous blood so that the latter is warmed as it enters the body, the arterial blood is cooled, and the limb extremity loses less heat to the outside. This adaptation is found in waders and gulls as well as in more aquatic birds and in the flippers of aquatic mammals such as seals. Of course, the limbs so adapted must be able to function efficiently at low temperatures, and there are other, more complex mechanisms which make this possible.

Behavioural modifications must also take place in an animal's general adaptation to its environment. We have already noted migratory adaptations which remove birds from the extreme problem of the arctic winter. But the short summer season also necessitates appropriate behavioural adjustments. There is little time for courtship for example, and the breeding displays must be well-developed by the time the birds arrive in the north. There is only time for one brood of young, and there must be no delay in egg-laying, incubation, and rearing of those young. The American robin for example, which elsewhere takes around 13 days to rear the young, manages to achieve this in 9 days in the tundra. This is made possible by the long hours of daylight and the almost ad lib food supply. Robins may be seen feeding young for up to 21 hours in the day.

Among the gregarious bird species of the north, all of them aquatic, display is a communal affair, as elsewhere and, as is usual in aquatic birds, the breeding adornments are largely confined to the head and upper parts. It is little use having adornments or recognition marks which are under water. The male eider is a slight exception with its delicate rose-pink breast, but it is the exception that proves the rule, for the eider drake display includes a rearing up in the water so that the gorgeous breast is fully revealed, while the bird emits a loud "whoo-hooooo" like an avian wolf-whistle.

Among the less social species such as the various passerines, or perching birds, including the sparrows and robins already mentioned and a few others such as water pipits and horned larks, the displays are much reduced. Males still display to females and sing in territory, but the performance does not have the frantic flavour typical of territorial display in more temperate regions. In the latter there is competition for space and for food whereas in the tundra there is plenty of both to go round.

In these and other ways the birds and other animals of the tundra are so well adapted to life in the northern summer that they would probably be uncomfortable elsewhere. Many such adaptations take innumerable generations to evolve and are then very deep-seated and resistant to change. There are also the short-term modifications by means of which an individual animal becomes fitted to, say, a particular level of temperature or humidity. Humans can adjust to their surroundings in both ways and we, like the Eskimos, were comfortable enough once we had the proper clothing. The main item in this is the thick one-piece Eskimo parka, broadly open at the bottom for freedom of movement, with a big fur-edged hood and a draw-string around the neck. The draw-string is for altering the diameter of the neck-hole, letting warm air flow up and out when one is too hot, or keeping it in when cold. In the tundra summer our usual problem was overheating, for the Eskimo parkas are very efficient. But we had

A king eider in breeding dress

to keep them on as protection against the mosquitoes.

Similarly, the birds and mammals of the tundra have a covering of fur or feathers which can be kept closed to trap warm air next to the skin, or opened up to let out excess heat. And it too forms a protection against the mosquitoes and other biting flies which are thereby forced to concentrate on areas of relatively bare skin around the eyes and, in mammals, ears. In us they had the rest of the face and hands to play with and took advantage accordingly, as I describe later.

The Eskimos of today, or perhaps yesterday, are adapted physically, physiologically, and psychologically to their environment to a remarkable degree. Not only are they stocky of build - a good shape for reducing heat loss - and swarthy of complexion for protection against the large amount of ultra-violet light reflected off ice, snow, and water, they also have the right attitude to their environment. They accept it for what it is: harsh in many ways but pleasant enough if you go along with it and adapt, instead of fighting it and trying to mould it to your prejudices. In this philosophy they developed the parka, a fine protection against most of the environmental perils without being restrictive to normal movement, and easily removed indoors where the flies and wind cannot bite.

Shortly after our second arctic summer I had the enormous privilege of attending an informal celebration in honour of the 80th birthday of the great arctic explorer and scholar Vilhjalmur Stefansson. Most of the people present were old arctic hands compared with me and were dancing, drinking, or enjoying the other rituals common to informal parties, whereas I was more interested in sitting at the feet of the great man so that I might gather a few pearls of wisdom. He was fascinating. And also kindly. It was quite a large party; in a country farmhouse, in the Canadian winter; with too many guests to stay the night in conventional comfort. The great man asked where we were sleeping. I explained, truthfully, that I, at least, would rather sleep in the hay barn under a polar bear skin than in a stuffy room full of people. "Anyway" I said "I've got my Eskimo parka". His eyes lit up. "Go and get it" he said " - I'll show you how we used to live in the north!" Then, rather to his young wife's embarrassment, he stripped to the waist, donned my parka and stood, an island of quiet satisfaction amid the clamour of loosening inhibitions.

The single, movable layer of insulation is by far the best covering for the artic environment. The Eskimos, by a combination of thought, and trial and error, have simply repeated the adaptations evolved by other animals through ages of natural selection. Nowadays the Eskimo clothes are made of duffle cloth from the Hudson's Bay stores, and the trousers may be blue jeans, but the principle of one windproof layer is still the best one to follow. When the clothing was made of caribou skin one could sit out on the ice for hours fishing, or waiting for seals to surface, without feeling cold. This is not nearly so easy in our more "advanced" garments, unless they are good functional copies of Eskimo clothes. I have never been as cold as I was in our first season when I had to make do with what winter clothes I already had. Several layers of woollies and European parkas were much less efficient than the single Eskimo parka I acquired later. More modern arctic gear demonstrates the lesson learnt from the natives, the quilted, synthetic, waterproof parkas and anoraks being good copies of the skin or duffle Eskimo parka, just as long as they are not restricting, have no fastenings for the wind to sneak through, can be adjusted to let warm air out and cool air in - or, of course, kept completely closed - and have a substantial hood to protect the face.

Head and footgear are just as important as the other clothes and here too we see the beauty and simplicity of successful adaptation. The Eskimo hood is large, covering the head in a great monk's cowl, with a fringe of fur. This fringe is not simply for decoration. Its function is to give a soft edge to the hood, on which moisture from one's breath will not condense and freeze. Wolverine is best for this, but fox and dog are good too. There is still plenty of fur trapping done in the north and I was able to get parkas with fox fur around the hood, as well as with the usual Eskimo decorations of ric-rac around the cuffs and bottom edge. The Eskimo has a very nice sense of design, derived no doubt from his closeness to nature.

This sense of design is nowhere seen better than in the Eskimo bobble hat or tuque. This is a close-fitting crocheted or knitted hat with tall sides and a floppy top from which hangs a substantial tassel on a short cord. One wonders why a tassel? Well, the great fur-fringed hood is in fact too big and floppy at the front to stand out from the brow, falling, unless supported, over the eyes. The tassel on the tuque is so designed to lie exactly at the point under the front of the hood where it would otherwise fall over the brow, and thus supports the front of the hood in the most efficient way possible. It does this job much better than the peak of a cap or the brim of a conventional hat, both of which articles are easily displaced under the hood. I am inclined to think that this must be the origin of the bobble on a bobble hat.

Eskimo boots are made from caribou or seal skin according to usage and availability of materials. The feet are always fur side inside for utility but the legs may have fur side outside for decoration. Seal skin boots are best for rough or wet work, though nowadays they tend to be replaced by rubber wellingtons or insulated boots. In fact, much of the traditional Eskimo clothing is being replaced by western items of dress as the native population changes its way of life. The speed with which this change is taking place is far from beneficial to the Eskimo, the old way of life with its complex skills and other adaptations being lost before proper psychological and operational adjustment has been made to the new situation. On the whole this is very sad. It was extremely depressing to see, in some northern townships, the slum-like shacks inhabited by natives living on government hand-outs, and the spoilt kids sneaking into the Northern Affairs shed to help themselves to the individual cornflakes packets that a magnanimous but incredibly stupid administration had provided for them. This is not really the place to protest at bureaucratic malfunctioning. Anyone who is interested should read Farley Mowat's delightful book *Never Cry Wolf.*

Not all Eskimos have succumbed to the temptation of an easy life however. There were some in Ungava who resisted the debilitating influence of Government hand-outs, and in the Belcher Islands the population was largely isolated and had to be self-sufficient. In Ungava there was one outstanding example of Eskimo pride and independence in the marvellous form of one Joby Snowball, a dwarf, even by Eskimo standards, but owning his own Peterhead boat with chugging engine, and employing a native assistant. He lived by hunting and would not even take the official government assistance to which he was entitled. One day Joby steamed in to our camp on False River, racing through the shoals on the receding tide in a manner which we considered highly dangerous, to inspect these specimens of white madness who were up to something funny on the treeline. He was courteous and friendly and after the ice was broken by their few words of American and our fewer words of Eskimo we invited him to lunch on tea and bannock. "Eeeee" he said - "Yes". But then: "hold it!" he gestured and strode off (he was all in proportion, though a dwarf) to his boat, returning with an enormous salmon in his arms

from which he cut four proud steaks which Nic broiled over the fire. That was a meal to remember. It would have cost a week's wages in a city eatery. And each party found the other amusing.

The Eskimo in fact has a well-developed, even sophisticated sense of humour. After that meal we allowed ourselves the post-prandial indulgence of a comparison of firearms - an exchange common to hunters everywhere. I proudly displayed my old, heavy, but very accurate .22 martini action rifle and the Eskimos brought out their battered old bolt action .22s. We stood a can up on a rock of course and displayed our prowess. Except for Nic that is. He was at that time far from being a marksman and stood in the background in a sort of subliminal sulk. But then he suddenly brightened up. He always had a bizarre sense of humour, which gave us much mutual enjoyment. Rushing to his tent he brought out our double-barrelled 12 bore shotgun and with its spread shot proceeded to blast the daylight out of, or rather through, the target. Everyone was delighted.

Eskimos enjoy any kind of slapstick. They will roll around with delight if anyone falls in the water, as long as there is no danger. But sometimes their sense of humour is much more subtle. In the Belcher Islands I became very friendly with one of the Eskimos from the local camp; the leading hunter of the group, named Noah (note the missionary influence in the names). Noah often came to our camp and I found that he knew every bird and mammal of the area, the different sexes, where and how they bred, what their habits were, and much more. He knew it all as the city dweller knows the inanimate objects in his largely artificial environment. Noah was fascinated by my work with the ducklings. I explained to him that they weren't afraid of me because they thought I was their mother, and he used to bring his little boy and sit at a respectful distance watching while I waded in the ponds with my brood.

One day while Noah was sitting quietly watching, a strange party of Eskimos arrived in a Peterhead boat and Noah went off to

see them. Later he came back with one of them, much to my annoyance, for he knew I didn't like other people around the place for they could easily disturb my work. But Noah stood at a discreet distance with the stranger, talking to him earnestly. I must reveal that the stranger was simple-minded; a genuine Eskimo E.S.N. Noah simply couldn't resist it. "Look" he said, pointing proudly towards me where I stumbled through the pond with my ducklings. "Look – he's their mother!" The expression on the stranger's face was indescribable.

Earlier that season we had been somewhat taken aback ourselves; in a situation which illustrates the varieties of taste in northern clothing. After we had been dropped in the Belchers by the Canso flying boat and had set up our tents on the lake shore, the weather blew up and we were stormbound. There were four of us; two colleagues having flown in the day before on a fisheries expedition. There we were, all in our Eskimo gear – duffle parkas with fur-fringed hoods, Eskimo tuques, fur mittens, the lot. But someone must have seen the Canso come down, for the next day there appeared on the horizon three figures. As they came nearer we could see peaked caps and leather jackets; then blue jeans and rubber boots; and then broad grins on the swarthy faces of three Eskimos.

At this point I cannot resist relaying to my captive audience – if you are still there, that is – another of my favourite tundra tales. When we were in the north the boom in Eskimo art was just beginning. People in general were beginning to recognise the remarkable Eskimo talent for art, particularly sculpture. As a result the output of Eskimo sculpture was increasing and a lot of junk coming onto the market. But it was still possible to find good pieces at not too prohibitive a price, and at one Hudson's Bay

Noah, an Eskimo with whom the author became friendly. Relatively untouched by western civilisation he seemed very contented despite the lack of amenities that most people would consider essential

stores I had acquired two exquisite soapstone carvings – a walrus and a Canada goose. In the Belchers we were able to barter for carvings; tobacco, tea, and ammunition being good currency. In this way I added a few pieces, of varying quality, to my modest collection.

But I couldn't find one specific piece that I particularly wanted: a seal lying on its side with head and hind flippers up – "playing gravy boats" as one of my friends has delightfully put it. Now Joe, Noah's eldest son, had no sculptural work in hand, so I talked him into doing this particular piece for me. And in order to make sure he knew exactly what I wanted I lay down on the ground in basking seal posture – "just like this" I said. Two days later Joe brought me the carving, grinning, perhaps a little more than usual. It was just what I had asked for: a lovely, chunky little seal in just the right posture. Moreover, one could tell it was a cow seal. It was very obviously pregnant.

Many people are puzzled to find such sophisticated art and humour in races they would normally regard as savages. Yet advanced technology and high standards of spending are by no means essential to a successful life. The "primitive" Eskimo is adapted to his harsh, flat environment just as well, probably better, than so-called civilised man is to high-rise apartment living.

Every organism lives at a certain point on the general ecological scale of size. The kind of effect that the elements have on an animal, and the animal's adaptations to those elements, vary with the animal's size. As humans, we become accustomed to certain geographical features in our everyday environment. When moved to a different environment – say from town to country, or vice versa – one feels a natural agoraphobia or claustrophobia according to the direction of change. One gets used to orienting and route-finding by reference to obvious landmarks of a particular size: hills or ranges of hills, houses or blocks of them, trees or woods, paths or intersections, fences, walls, and hedges. Thus, when first isolated in the "flat, featureless tundra" I felt lost because there were apparently no landmarks. Then gradually I got used to orienting by different coloured boulders or patches of vegetation, by ponds of different shape or depth, by a stranded icefloe or skeleton, or by a low bluff in the distance instead of a hill.

With a small range of size of vertical features – boulders, rises, or bluffs – one is out of sight of home in a very short time – exactly as one can be out of sight of land in a small boat only 100 yards from shore if it is being tossed around in a swell, the troughs of which are so deep that you cannot see over the crests. One may rise to the crest of the wave, or bluff, from time to time, but the glimpse of home is fleeting, and in some way increases the feeling of isolation.

In the tundra, as in other types of terrain, the vegetation under one's feet is a forest to its indigenous fauna. There they are hidden in a living maze, sheltered from the wind and protected from rapid changes of temperature. And they can take even more effective cover immediately they are threatened by storm or enemy. We, on the other hand, trundling along on our hind legs like mobile skyscrapers, are exposed to all the perils the greater environment has to offer. The wind is a particularly important factor in all this. As in maritime or desert areas, the wind cuts the tundra vegetation down to size, and with it the animals, including Man.

The mice can burrow; the insects can lose themselves amongst the vegetation, leaf litter, or pebbles; the sparrows – country cousins of the house sparrow – can shelter behind stones or clods; the hares and grouse are protected by small boulders. But the human has to crouch, or lie down and curl up, to take advantage of whatever natural protection the terrain has to offer. Thus, in a howling wind which blows through one's clothing and wits, the insects are grounded. But in the lee of a bluff or boulder pile they find a protected area as big – relatively speaking – as the Albert Hall or Yankee Stadium, and there they may continue to indulge in their dances and competitions, like the humans in their artificial enclosures.

And so, if one is going to live in isolation, or semi-isolation, one has to accept the dominance of the elements, and adapt. The Eskimo garments, for example, are adaptations to their environment – as I have already explained – but so is their behaviour. The wise tundra dweller avoids the areas and times of day which produce the most mosquitoes. And in the winter he does not emulate the mad dogs and Englishmen who go out in the midnight sun, face forward to the icy blast, ever onward until death – or at least frostbite – puts an end to their folly. No; he takes cover when the elements are at their roughest, and ventures out with caution, keeping his face out of the biting wind beneath his ample hood.

But this does not imply a miserably harsh existence. In fact, the wilderness is the kindest of teachers because of its unyielding powers which force one to be efficient. Under effective conditions of isolation one has to be physically and psychologically self-reliant, or perish. Thus one adapts by integration into the way

Making camp, Labrador, in our first season. June 5th

of life of the tundra, or whatever. This condition – this state of "belonging" as an integrated part of the multi-dimensional ecological web, giving and taking as a unit in the mutualistic environmental complex – is what all the earliest peoples experienced after the human race had evolved from our more ape-like ancestors. We inherited it as part of our place in an ongoing environmental concern. It involves an adaptability and self-sufficiency which we discard at our peril. And it is a prime example of the old saying that an influence must often be cruel to be kind.

Thus, to Nic and me, left in the middle of the nowhere of Quebec-Labrador, our motto was not "excelsior!" – though this could well apply to our scientific programme – but "adapt!" And adapt we had to, for the very first night after our Eskimo friends left us we had a blizzard which demonstrated that Nic's tent was not as resistant to the elements as we had been led to believe. In the morning he was floating on his air mattress in a pool of snow water which had easily soaked through the roof but would not drain out through the groundsheet. So we had to build a hut.

Have you ever built a dry-stone wall? Well I dare say that a few

The author holding an arctic char, a rare delicacy at that time. Note the hut with dry stone walls and roof of tree trunks and turf

of you have; but have you tried it with rounded, wave-washed stones and boulders? And with a roof of tree trunks that had to be carried half a mile, and with turf and moss instead of tiles? Not that I can claim any pretensions of architectural grandeur for our construction. But it stayed up eventually. And at least it blended with the environment. On the other hand it was, I must admit, somewhat primitive. It served – well, tolerated – us for a couple of months, and was still standing when we left. But I like to think that in years to come, some fervent tundra archaeologist will discover it and go into printed raptures about the architecturally primitive nature of the natives who once inhabited that part of Quebec-Labrador.

In this, our first season, the significance of adaptability was brought home to us in a number of ways. We were both accustomed to living under what most people would regard as primitive conditions – though of course it all depends on one's definition of 'primitive' – and indeed preferred the wilderness to most other environments. But we were in the wilderness for a highly civilised purpose; the pursuit of a scientific endeavour which would take all our time and attention – all that wasn't spent on existing, that is. When, therefore, we found it more difficult to live off the land than we had expected – we found later that our chosen area had been heavily hunted over a short time before – we tried living on tea and bannock, as many Eskimos did during periods of game shortage. Now, bannock is the standby of the northlands adventurers, and a well-cooked bannock is a delight to nostril and palate and most soothing to an empty gut. Based on the good old Scottish bannock, it is simply a stiff mixture of flour and water, with a dash of baking powder and salt to taste, fried.

However, much to our chagrin we found that bannock two or three times a day palled somewhat. Even more disturbingly, we became listless and depressed and found it trying to perform even the simplest of camp chores. We had not ventured very far afield for food because of the time it would take from the scientific programme; and time was still a priority. Even our attempts at trapping rodents – for scientific purposes, using skins, skeletons, parasites, and population data – had been unsuccessful, for we were in a "crash" year with the population at the lowest ebb of its fluctuating four-year cycle. So we didn't even have "mice" to eat. They are quite palatable, like most animals, and we weren't subject to the peculiar food fads of most so-called 'civilised' people, so we would have eaten them readily. Probably with gusto.

We had an assortment of porcupine joints hanging up to dry in the wind, but we left them hanging in case of real emergency (actually, I suspect that subconsciously we didn't really fancy them). And we had discovered, rather to our suprise, that we couldn't stomach gull. We have since found that young gull, still in the down, is supposed to be quite palatable. And I even have one American naturalist friend who claims to have eaten adult gull with relish. But I fancy it must have been a different species from our glaucous gulls.

Anyway, there we were, sulking on tea and bannock, and simply not having the time to go out and tickle trout, stalk sparrows, or venture far to find game. And I steadfastly refused to shoot the few ducks that did appear in the vicinity; that would be like shutting the stable door before the horse was in there. We were in the North to study ducks and I would be damned if I would shoot our data!

The problem, therefore, was how to adapt to this particular and rather peculiar situation. On taking thought I decided, on the basis of our restricted diet and particular symptoms, that we were probably suffering from vitamin deficiency. This was relatively easy to remedy. Scattered through the tundra vegetation were growing vitamin supplies, already encapsulated in colourful, succulent-looking skins. Berries, of various kinds, were there for the picking. Man has achieved very little by his technology that natural selection, in time, has not evolved before him. The principle of super-attractive packing for promoting food consumption was evolved by plants millions of years before man was even hinted at in primate history, the seeds of succulent-fruited species being carried safely away inside animals and deposited, thoroughly fertilised, elsewhere. We simply had to take advantage of it. Some people would call this the bounty of nature. All we had to do was perceive the nature of the bounty, avoiding the few specimens we suspected were poisonous, and making a point of eating a hundred of the others per day as we went about our business. In a week we were well again. Whether we would have recovered regardless – I know not. We certainly felt better, both physically and psychologically.

The experimental field biologist is in a better position than most to appreciate the principles and practice of adaptation, for he is constantly surrounded by examples, some of which are much less credible than the wildest fiction. Even so, I was considerably astonished by a spider colony near our camp. It is not that I normally avoid spiders and so didn't know what to expect. On the contrary, I rather like them. A very handsome specimen kept me company in my tent all season, hanging above the door flap and doubtless feasting on the mosquitoes which penetrated my sanctum in spite of my efforts to dissuade them. And I had a beautiful little jumping spider, measuring some three inches claw to claw, that hung up in a special glass-fronted cage back in my lab., ready to leap upon the flies I caught for him. Admittedly, I didn't feel completely friendly towards the tarantulas I kept, for they could dart upon my hand faster than I could remove it from their cage when feeding them. But on the whole I rather approve of spiders. We would be pretty fly-blown without them.

Our astonishing tundra spiders hung about on the bluff we soon named "Spider Cliff". Their orb-webs clustered its overhang in scores, varying greatly in size but all built, of course, on the same pattern – the same, as far as we could tell, as the good old English garden spider web. As in the Royal Academy, suitable hanging space was definitely at a premium, and there were webs in front of webs in front of webs. Each one had its life-line to a crevice in the rock, and each one was likely to contain at its centre, whatever the

Nic on spider cliff. The river served as our water supply

weather, a fat and presumably – in its own arachnoid way – contented spider.

Nothing remarkable about that you might think. But when we arrived there that cliff was covered in snow. Snow that must have been there for nine months. And a week after the snow had gone the cliff was festooned with the delicate symmetry of the spiders' food traps. Those spiders had been nine months in hibernation and yet, as soon as the snow had melted, their midget brains were able to organise their other organs to fashion a structure of a standard of subtle and delicate efficiency beyond the abilities of most humans. The orb-web is incredible enough, but for the orb-web builder to be able to adapt to spending most of its life under snow was something we had not expected.

The more we studied these spiders – as I explain elsewhere we studied them in some detail because of a serious shortage of ducks – the more attached to them we became. Even animals as lowly as these in the Animal Kingdom can be seen to have individual behavioural peculiarities when one gets to know them well enough, and the carefully-recorded daily activities of Fred, Marmalade, and the rest, acquired an increasing interest for us as the days passed.

The mosquitoes that covered us also served as food for the ducklings

The spiders were our particular friends because they ate so many mosquitoes. And the mosquitoes provided our most significant lesson in adaptation for survival; not because of what happened to them but because of what they did to us. The dominant organism in the tundra is not Man, nor the wolf, but the mosquito. In countless millions per square mile the mosquitoes, with their smaller cousins the black-flies, totally dominate life in the summer, forcing one to adapt to them, leave, or go mad. Some people say the black-flies are the worst, some the mosquitoes. It probably depends on the thickness of one's skin, physical and psychological, and one's relative biochemical sensitivity to the bites of the different insects. I happen to be particularly sensitive, biochemically, to the bite of the mosquito. This beast is what is known in entomological circles as a "piercer and sucker". Like many of its relatives it obtains its daily bread in liquid form, piercing some innocent provider with its proboscis and sucking up a rich blood soup. But first it must inject an anticoagulant to prevent the blood from clotting in its throat, as it were, and it is this chemical to which I am sensitive. I don't mind the discomfort of the bites, and one can become accustomed to myriads of mosquitoes crawling over one all the time, but the injections can knock me out. And they itch like mad. The black-flies didn't bother me — they feed in a somewhat different manner — but the irritation set up by dozens of daily mosquito bites on my ankles and shins resulted in permanent scars from the scratching thereof.

You may be wondering why shins and ankles. Well, that was the only region of one's anatomy where they could reach the skin through the clothing. Our hands and faces had to be permanently anointed with fly-dope — insect-repellant of a, thankfully, effective type, so the beasts couldn't take an unobstructed meal. But around the ankles the clothing was closely applied to the body where the trousers were tucked into socks. And this is where they got us. They had to penetrate thick socks, corduroy or drill trousers, and wollen long johns, but that seemed to put them on their mettle for they certainly succeeded.

These particular mosquitoes are quite large, as one can see from the photograph of a few on Nic's arm. This picture was taken on a particularly bad day when the mosquitoes were a real problem, and Nic is wearing a head net — a protection we had to adopt on those days when the insects seemed to ignore the fly dope. I approached Nic to take a picture of an impressive covering of mosquitoes, but my arrival scared them away and very few came back — a rather unusual state of affairs. But my picture of a minimal covering of mosquitoes can give you an idea of what it is

A moderate covering of mosquitoes on sleeve

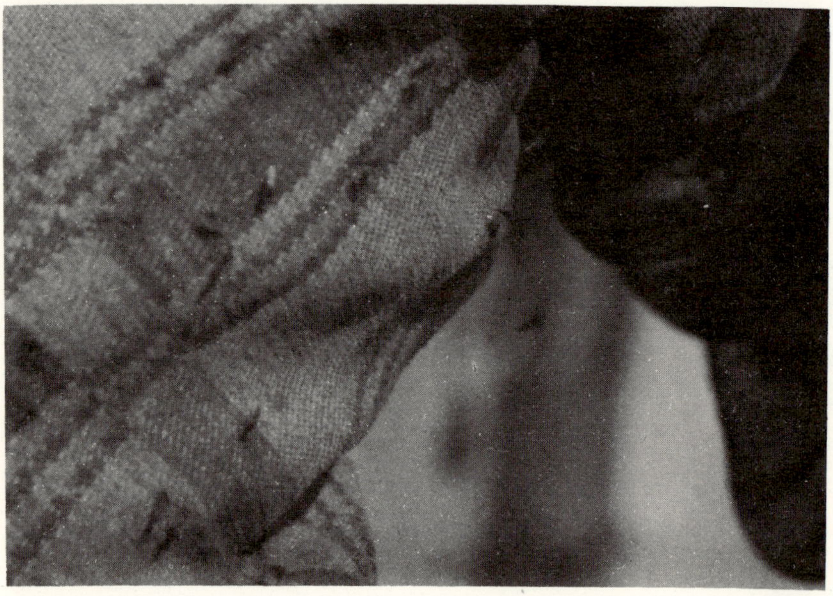

like when there are plenty of them.

The mosquito menace has of course given rise to a considerable folk-lore in the north. On our way in we were regaled with a number of gleefully-gruesome stories by a friendly Hudson's Bay store manager – such as the one about the time a mosquito landed on the local airstrip and was loaded up with petrol before they realised what it was. Such stories indicate the respect with which the locals, including the Eskimos, regard these insects. Dogs certainly seem to have succumbed to excessive piercing and sucking, and even experienced tundra workers are occasionally tent-bound on bad days. If by some mischance we were to be deposited in the north with only one civilised aid to survival we would certainly choose fly-dope.

In order to work in the north therefore one has to come to terms with the mosquito. Given the protection of fly-dope this largely involves psychological adaptation. One simply has to come to terms with the fact that one is going to be covered in mosquitoes most of the time, and have them buzzing in one's eyes and ears and mouth even when one is eating. Nevertheless one retains a profound dislike of the beasts, and we were inclined to gloat when we found a specimen infested with an unpleasant-looking red parasite.

There were of course breaks in the daily mosquito misery. In the cool of morning and evening there were a few minutes of respite, and similarly during rain or high winds. And we would occasionally have the luxury of a lift in a passing outboard-powered canoe, when we would accelerate out into the centre of the lake leaving the mosquitoes behind.

For one glorious week after the break-up of the ice, before the adult mosquito emerges from the pupal case at the water surface, one can roam the tundra with relative ease. And there is a similar period at the end of the summer as the nights get colder and the mosquitoes die of insectal old age. But in between there seem to be more mosquitoes than all the rest of the fauna put together. And indeed there might be, for there is something like a million square miles of fresh water lakes, rivers, and tundra pools in Canada, with a considerable population of mosquito larvae and pupae under more than half of it.

As an interesting exercise in biological mind-boggling I like to try to imagine the numbers of mosquito young swimming in this mass of water or frozen under the ice. Let us say, at a conservative estimate, that there are only 10 individuals for every cubic foot of water; that the water is on average only 2 feet deep; and that only half a million square miles of Canadian water contains mosquitoes. If my mathematics are correct, this makes nearly 28 million potential mosquitoes per square mile. This is probably a considerable underestimate. And there are probably just as many other annoying insects including greenbottles and bluebottles, as well as the black-flies. And the aquatic species don't stay over the patch of water where they first experience adulthood. They congregate on suitable clumps of vegetation waiting for the aroma of a perambulating food supply, on detection of which they fly up the scent gradient like wasps to a jam pot.

It is a salutary thought that the single insect Order – the Diptera – to which all these beasts belong is probably the dominant animal group in the northern lands. Certainly, if it weren't for the "flies" the tundra lands of Canada and Alaska would become one enormous summer holiday camp. Arctic mosquitoes do not, fortunately, harbour the malarial parasite but, nevertheless, a fortune awaits the developer of an economic means of dealing with the tundra flies. We should remember that over much of the earth's surface we are not actually, only potentially, the dominant organism.

Amid such occupational hazards in the wilderness a sense of humour is rather important, almost as important to the Eskimo perhaps as the other adaptations to environment. It was certainly useful to Nic and me. And our nonsensical predilections in this respect probably enabled us to see the funny side of things particularly easily. There is considerable evidence that level of intelligence and sense of humour are closely connected, and that the enjoyment of nonsensical humour, for example that of Edward Lear, Lewis Carroll, and the Goons, indicates an advanced development. Chesterton in fact believed, and I am sure he was right, that a feeling for nonsense is correlated with a sense of values and religious wonder. I therefore ask no pardon for taking a brief look at the way in which we occasionally relaxed in the north.

In his early arctic days Nic was not very well organised in his camp chores. He was, after all, only 18 years old; and he has since become an outstanding field man. I was a hard task master and expected Nic to quickly learn to do things as well as I could. But the first month of the first season was somewhat disorganised. Eventually, when Nic served up cold, burnt porage at 11 a.m. I decided something had to be done. But it had to be tactful. So I went into a "Nic getting breakfast" routine, humming the first few phrases of a blues tune over and over and over while falling in the fire, tripping over my feet, plates, and cook pots, spilling water and dropping cutlery in a complex culinary caricature. Nic was convulsed, and the results were beneficial to us both.

Our interest in nonsense often blossomed – if that is the right word – into verse. We worked well together, having the same streak of intellectual madness, and one of our best efforts will serve to close this chapter. One evening I offered Nic an idea for another poem. It was called *Haggis,* but I only had the first line and the metre. At the end of breakfast the next day Nic cleared his voice in the standard preparatory manner and shuffled his feet. We had been silent up until then as I'm always very touchy first thing in the morning and we had a "no talking 'til after breakfast" agreement. "O.K." I said "let's have it". Here, after suitable polishing, is what emerged:

Haggis extinct? Never!
The suggestion should never occur.
Why, I found a wee nest in the heather,
That was lined with a Haggis's fur,
And a note on the door saying "Back around four"
And a little green mouse with a hat in each paw.

My reaction of course was quite normal,
There's really no more to be said,
I gave him a bun – I only had one –
And patted him over the head,
Saying "terribly rude – he ought to be sued,
To go off and leave you without any food".

The mouse then adjusted his whisker
And smoothed out a crease in his brow;
Said "I really don't mind, he's often quite kind,
But his wife is a bloated old cow!"
"Tut-tut, my young rat, though she may be fat,
You never should speak of a lady like that!"

The mouse took a pinch from his snuffbox,
While blushing as red as a beet;
Said "When she comes in she picks up the bin
And bundles me in by my feet!"
"Ho-ho" I retorted, "I might have thought it:
If I'd seen her do it you bet she'd have caught it!"

The evening was drawing quite close then,
Twas beginning to get rather dark,
So although he was vexed I paid my respects
And caught the last bus from the Park.
These juvenile mice are really quite nice;
I'm glad I was able to give him advice.

Haggis extinct? Never!

3 Eider Natural History

The eider duck, *Somateria mollissima,* around which this book is written, is a bird known to most people as a name – in "eiderdown" – but not as an animal in its own right. To tell the truth, many people find it not a very handsome bird on first sight, with its bulky clumsiness on land and its peculiar facial profile with little of a "forehead", but like any other animal it is seen to have a fascination of its own when acquaintance becomes more intimate. The drake in breeding plumage is very handsome indeed, with beautiful pastel colours on head and neck, contrasting pleasingly with the black and white of the rest of the plumage, and its display calls are most attractive – particularly when heard in

European eider drakes in full breeding dress

the natural environment against the background of the sounds of the sea, or in that magical stillness which falls over that environment from time to time every season. I shall long remember one strangely silent day in the Labrador tundra when the only sounds were the wing-whinings of the mosquitoes and the crooning of eider drakes way out of sight down river.

In the water the eider is transformed from a clumsy waddler to a master of its environment. It can swim suprisingly fast at the surface, dive with ease and incredible speed, and swim beneath the surface with grace and agility. It is indeed a "diving duck" belonging to one of the groups of ducks which have taken advantage, over evolutionary time, of the rich supply of food available beneath the surface at depths inaccessible to their more staid cousins the surface-feeders or "dabbling" ducks.

As a species the eider has an interesting distribution around the northern fringes of the habitable world, from the tundra to the temperate climatic zones. There is a discontinuity in its distribution in the northern part of Eurasia, probably as a result of the establishment of separate North Atlantic and North Pacific centres of dispersal after the most recent of the ice ages. Five different geographical forms or subspecies of the eider are recognised, but there seems to be little interchange of individuals between the Atlantic and Pacific populations and the subspecies remain geographically and structurally distinct. In western Europe, at least, the eider is increasing in numbers and extending its range southwards. It first bred in the Netherlands in 1906, and now appears regularly in the Mediterranean, principally at the mouth of the Rhone.

The eider, or "common eider", is placed with its nearest relatives, the king eider, spectacled eider, and Steller's eider, all arctic species, in the Tribe Somateriini, or, by some authors, with the saw-billed ducks in the Tribe Mergini. The common eider is the biggest of the eider group, almost as large as a small goose. The male is basically black beneath and white above, with a white patch on the flanks and black on the top of the head. The female is the drab brown colour typical of the female sex in ducks, principally for camouflage when on the nest. At close quarters however the female's plumage is seen to be quietly attractive, with warm brown feathers streaked and mottled with dark, almost black markings. The male in breeding plumage has beautiful patches of lime green on the sides of the upper neck extending forwards above the cheek region to below and behind the eye. He also has a delicate wash of creamy-pink on the breast and lower

The eiders of the world drawn by Peter Scott. Reproduced by permission of Royle Publications, publishers of A Coloured Key to the Wildfowl of the World

Heads of male and female American eider

neck, and, as one would expect, it is this head, neck and breast region which is shown to advantage during the breeding displays, the head being thrown up and back to varying degrees and the breast displayed in ritualised postures.

Variations between the subspecies of the common eider are to be seen largely in the head region of the male, principally concerning the shape and colour of the bill and the general profile of the head. The females of the different subspecies can be distinguished however, once one knows them well, and I was interested to find that even the colour of the nest down was different in the two subspecies we studied in the Canadian tundra.

The "type" subspecies of the common eider – the one that was described first – is the European eider *Somateria mollissima mollissima*. The scientific name is well-chosen, for the generic term *Somateria* comes from the Greek *somatos,* meaning body, and *erion,* meaning wool or down; and *mollissima,* from the Latin, means very soft. The European eider is one of the larger subspecies, with a body about 58cm (23") long. It breeds in Iceland, northern Britain, Scandinavia, and east to Novya Zemlya, usually, like the other common eiders, along the coasts or on offshore islands, and sometimes inland around lakes or on islands in rivers. It is basically resident in the breeding areas all the year round, as long as there is open water, but some individuals move south in winter.

The Faeroe eider *S. m. faeroeensis* is the smallest of the

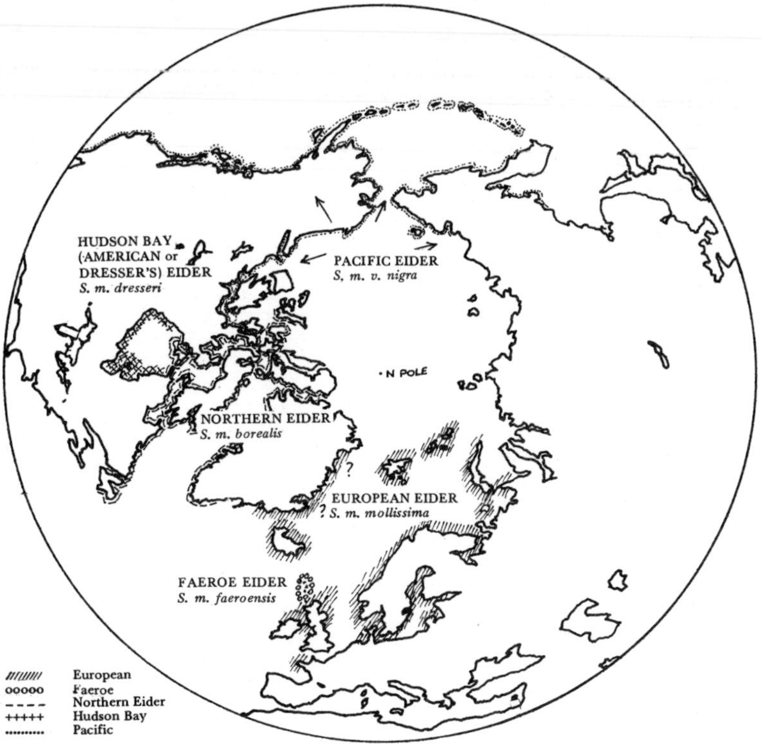

World distribution of the Common Eider. Note that for many areas information is scanty, in some areas there is overlap of populations, and in a few regions – eg – East Greenland – information is quite inadequate.

subspecies, resident in the Faeroe Islands. Except for size it is very similar to the European eider, with the same greenish-coloured bill. Moving westwards we then find the northern eider *S. m. borealis* which breeds in west Greenland and the north-eastern coasts of Canada as far west as the north-west coast of Hudson Bay and northwards wherever there is open water. This is a medium-sized subspecies with a yellow rather than green bill. In the north-western parts of its range it meets and overlaps in distribution with the Pacific eider *S. m. v-nigra,* so-called because of the V-shaped black mark on the throat. This is the biggest of the subspecies and has a more orange bill. It breeds on islands and coastlines from the North-West Territories of Canada and westwards through Alaska, the Aleutian chain of islands, and north-eastern Asia. Then there is a gap in the distribution of the common eider in the central region of the arctic coastline of the U.S.S.R., the subspecies occurring next as we move westwards being the European eider, as mentioned above. The northern and Pacific eiders that breed in the coldest of the high arctic regions have to move out in the winter when everything freezes up, the northern eiders moving south, and the Pacific eiders of northern Canada moving westwards around the coast of Alaska to the open waters of the Bering Sea and the Aleutian Islands – a journey of up to 2,000 miles. Finally we have the American eider – sometimes called the Hudson Bay or Dresser's eider – *S. m. dresseri,* which breeds on the coasts of Hudson Bay and eastern Labrador. It is a medium-sized subspecies with a greenish bill, but the head profile is noticeably more rounded than in the other subspecies and the leathery backward continuations of the upper bill proceed much farther up towards the eye. The Labrador populations of the American eider migrate southwards down the Atlantic coast in the winter, but the Hudson Bay populations are largely sedentary, staying throughout the winter in leads in the ice kept open by fast-flowing currents along the west coast of the Bay and around islands to the east and north.

The northern eider also will stay in the high arctic during the winter as long as there are currents or tide-rips to keep the water open, and like the American eider can survive when the air temperature is 50 degrees below zero Fahrenheit. This is indeed remarkable, but the water temperature is considerably higher, for salt water freezes at about 28 degrees above zero. Even so, the general winter conditions are very severe and one can see why eiders have such excellent down insulation.

The eider is a strongly maritime species, spending most of the time at sea except during the breeding season. It is quite at home in rough water and may be found well out to sea in winter. It feeds however in shallow waters off low-lying muddy or sandy shores and rocky coastlines, diving for a variety of food organisms, largely animals. The eider's principal feeding adaptations are for the capture and digestion of molluscs – particularly the edible mussel – and any slow-moving animals, for example crustaceans such as crabs, that it can catch. Thus it has a very strong bill for grasping its prey, and an extremely muscular gizzard – the second part of the stomach in birds – for grinding up the hard-shelled animals which form such a large proportion of its prey. As in other birds with well-developed gizzards, small stones and gravel are swallowed and retained in the gizzard to assist this process. The grinding action of the gizzard on resistant prey such as mussel shells can be heard from outside the bird, in suitable conditions, and the gravel content of the gizzard may be as much as 15 per

Male and female European eiders drinking from a brackish pool

cent of the total. Otherwise, about 95 per cent of the food material is animal, a very large proportion of which – 50 to 90 per cent – consists of molluscs.

The capacity of the eider's gullet and gizzard is remarkable, the remains of 185 mussel shells having been found in one bird. But these were in various stages of disintegration, and a clearer picture is given by the gut contents of another bird whose gullet contained 11 whole mussels averaging about 1½" by 1" in size and whose gizzard contained 6 more specimens only slightly smaller and the remains of 7 more.

The favoured prey animals of the eider are found in the shallow waters of the littoral zone – between high and low water marks – and a few fathoms below. Normally they dive in 2 to 3 fathoms of water, but they can dive to 8 or 10 fathoms if necessary. Feeding dives vary in duration from a few seconds to around 50 seconds. The eider's speed and manouevrability under water are assisted by the development of a lobe on the hind toe, as in the mergansers. This gives an extra propulsive area to the webbed feet, and in the eider the lobe is very well developed, being half as wide as it is long. Also, the eider frequently uses the half-opened wings under water to assist propulsion, particularly when swimming down to the bottom and when the currents are strong. I call this "wing-swimming".

Sometimes when feeding under water an eider may almost literally "bite off more than it can chew", a few specimens having been found with a large mussel tightly clamped around the bird's tongue. A mussel can stay closed for long periods, and birds thus caught may half suffocate, half starve to death. But such occurrences are the exception and the eider's feeding mechanisms are highly efficient, as evidenced by their increase in numbers when not predated by man. The size of prey that an eider can in fact deal with is indicated by a record of Millais, the great naturalist-painter, who shot an eider with what appeared to be a long stick projecting from its bill. It was in fact a razor shell, 10″ long and 3″ in circumference. As the bird seemed perfectly healthy it was presumably having an unusually long meal!

Eider ducklings of course have to take smaller prey, as detailed

European eider female with brood of young ducklings

European eider female on nest with recently hatched ducklings

in chapter 6, beginning with small insects and crustaceans and gradually moving on to small and then bigger and bigger molluscs. The ducklings are dark brown to grey-brown above, according to subspecies, with a lighter streak stretching from the base of the bill over and behind the eye. The underparts are lighter brown or grey, palest on the belly. From a few days old they, like the adults, are quite at home in the water, diving and feeding in wave conditions that one would think were much too rough for such delicate creatures. But once beneath the surface they are, of course, in relatively calm water, and the adult females tend not to lead them into the water when the conditions are too adverse.

Eiders nest on low-lying coastlines, islands, and skerries, sometimes higher up inland around lakes, but always near water. This is because the young have to quickly learn to feed themselves on aquatic animals, the parents, as in other ducks, taking no part in the feeding of the young except for leading them to suitable feeding areas and protecting them, as far as they are able, from predators and adverse weather conditions.

The nest itself is made – by the female only – in a hollow in the ground, with a foundation of grasses, seaweeds, and other plants, plentifully lined with the down which is the eider down of commerce, and feathers. The nests are often placed in the open, the female being well camouflaged and difficult to detect when sitting tight and still on the nest, but not infreqently – presumably in areas where predation is a serious problem – they are partially or wholly concealed amongst or under rocks or vegetation. I have found nests under dwarf willow bushes, hidden amongst boulders, under fallen tree stumps, and concealed in tufts of sedges. In regions where ground cover is very sparse – as on the skerries from which we obtained our eggs in the Belcher Islands – every tuft of vegetation may conceal a nest. As we approached these low-lying shingle-covered rocks they seemed to be devoid of life except for the few scattered clumps of sedges. But as we landed on the shingle every clump produced a female eider who scuttered or flew away to the water close by. We had found no nests on the main part of the island where we were camped. Obviously, predation pressures had forced the birds off the main island masses to these isolated islets where the foxes could not get at them. The Eskimos knew they were there but were presumably well-enough supplied with food not to have to make the journey to collect eggs.

We see then that eiders may nest close together. In fact they form large nesting colonies when conditions are suitable, the big colony in the Thule district of Greenland for example containing up to 10,000 nests. This colonial nesting habit has, in part, led to the development of the eider down industries, large amounts of down being available from one area in a relatively short time.

Eiders not infrequently nest among colonies of arctic terns and other species of sea birds. The usual reason given for this is that the other species are much more efficient at driving away predators who are likely to take eggs or chicks at any opportunity. This is undoubtedly true, but there is another factor probably involved which concerns the "searching image" which predators are said to form inside their "minds" as an aid to finding prey. It would work roughly as follows: the gulls, which will take eggs of any species of bird if they can get them and are a serious problem to eiders all around the world, will build up a "searching image" for the eggs, young, and sitting adults of the terns or other birds which are usually the most numerous birds in mixed colonies with eiders. Thus they are more likely to miss the eider nests than they

Nests of American eider in Hudson Bay situated close together in mixed vegetation. The upper nest contains a double clutch. Such nests provided the author's study material

would if those nests were not in a mixed colony, for they will be "concentrating" on the dominant species for which they have a "searching image".

This spacing out of the eider nests, with the high degree of camouflage of the sitting eider, particularly when compared with a sitting tern, is an example of a "protean" phenomenon – a phenomenon which has developed, usually by natural selection, a high degree of unpredictability. To a gull, searching for nests in a mixed colony of eiders and terns, the occurrence of eider nests is unpredictable because it only has a "searching image" for terns' nests.

The eggs of the eider – large, olive-green eggs, usually 4 to 6 in a clutch – are normally covered with down by the female when she leaves the nest, except when she is sitting tight towards the end of the 28 day incubation period. Then she will stay until the last possible moment, often defaecating over the eggs as she leaves. This defaecation is probably, for the greater part, a self-protection mechanism, lightening her load for take-off. But it probably also has a useful side-effect in making the eggs less obvious or less attractive as food.

Other protean unpredictable defence mechanisms are used by both adult and young eiders. These, and many other examples of protean phenomena, are surveyed by David Humphries and myself in our forthcoming book *Protean Behavior* and I can only deal with them briefly here. As I have indicated, the female eider is largely a mobile brooder and protector for the young. Her principal method of protection of the young from predators is the well-known "injury-feigning" display in which she behaves in such a way that the predator, such as a fox, is led to believe that she is actually injured and follows her in expectation of an easy capture. This display occurs basically on land or across small patches of water when the young are still in or near the nest and in great danger from a predator such as a fox which could easily detect them by scent and sight if its attention was not distracted. The distraction display of injury feigning is such an accurate representation of the real thing that even humans are taken in by it, the displaying bird stumbling and flapping along if really incapacitated, occasionally falling over or stopping as if exhausted. Such a bird is of course in actual danger of being caught, and the protean, or unpredictable elements come into play in the unexpected changes of direction and actions which the displaying bird exhibits in an apparently natural manner, but which are so unpredictable in their occurrence and form as to effectively prevent the predator

Glaucous gull

from making its capture. Usually, when the predator has been decoyed far enough away from the young, which stay crouching on the ground or bunched in the water, the mother bird takes to the wing, or the water, and the family is eventually re-united.

Foxes, and sometimes polar bears, stoats, and weasels, are not the only enemies the ducklings have to fear however, for many birds will take ducklings as readily as they will eggs. Glaucous gulls and greater black-backed gulls, herring gulls and lesser black-backed gulls, skuas, ravens, and various birds of prey proper all relish ducklings at any time and will attack them on land or in the water. If the ducklings are in the water, however, they have something of an advantage, for they can crash dive, as explained later, disappearing beneath the surface in a fraction of a second. And here another protean phenomenon comes into play, for the ducklings usually start off in a loosely-bunched group and scatter beneath the surface. Thus an attacking bird will have no idea of where the prey it had its eye on is going to come up again; the pattern of scatter is unpredictable and confusing. But there are enemies in the water too: sharks and seals for example will readily snap up ducklings, and it says much for the defence mechanisms of adults and young when we realise that with an average clutch of five eggs once a year the common eider manages to maintain, or even increase its numbers.

It is in the very young ducklings that most eider mortality takes place. Hatching success is quite high, mammalian predators being dealt with by the sitting bird as already described, and avian predators seldom attacking eiders on the nest, partly because they are so well camouflaged and partly because they are quite powerful and defend themselves vigorously. Most adult birds and mammals, particularly the females, defend themselves most actively when they have a brood to care for, and eiders are no exception. For example, Dresser in 1871 described an instance of a raven actually attacking a female eider sitting on eggs. A considerable battle ensued and the raven may have won if the eider drake had not arrived on the scene and closed with the raven, the two birds eventually tumbling into an adjacent lake, at which point the raven of course had to disengage.

In the past, eiders' eggs have provided Eskimos with a valuable source of food in some areas, the eggs being collected in large numbers when fresh in May or June – the date depending upon the severity of the climate – and many of them eaten on the spot. But many more, often thousands if there were many Eskimos in the foraging party, would be hidden in safe places out of the sun until they became chilled in August and frozen in September, to provide a welcome article of food during the winter. Another method of dealing with them was to empty the contents, either direct or by squirting from the mouth, into tubes made from the intestines of walrus or seal. The resulting sausage made an excellent standby on hunting expeditions.

The skins of eiders have long been used by the Eskimos for making into blankets and clothing. Usually the outer feathers would be plucked from the skin leaving the downy covering, and the skins would be cured so that they were soft and pliable and then sewn together – with that wonderfully neat stitching practised by many Eskimo women even today – to make whatever article was needed. Sometimes the edges of blankets would be trimmed with the head skins of drake eiders and king eiders, and these must have been the most beautiful and efficient bed coverings ever made, for the best eider down is still the softest, warmest, and lightest insulating material known. The downy skins were also made into winter underwear – worn down side inside – and summer parkas, and must have been luxuriously comfortable. Today, such garments would be very expensive indeed on the open market. But the art seems to have been largely lost, though I did obtain – from the Hudson's Bay Store in Great Whale – a beautiful knick-knack holder like a mini-apron with four pockets, each pocket made from the cured head skin of an eider drake.

The principal significance of the eider to man has been the provision of down for the eider down industry. In Iceland and Norway such an industry thrived for many years and in Iceland at least it is still of considerable economic importance, though not as flourishing as in the past. In North America the industry was slower to get off the ground, the first such venture beginning in a small way on the north coast of the Gulf of St. Lawrence in 1933. Then in 1939 the Hudson's Bay Company obtained permission to begin a commercial eider down industry in southern Baffin Island.

In Iceland it has long been an offence against both the law and popular feeling to interfere with eiders, numerous "eider farms", particularly on small islands, having fields especially for the eiders to nest in. At one time the bigger farms could boast up to 12,000 nests or more, but now 6 or 7,000 is the maximum number of nests on any one farm.

The eiders are encouraged to breed by the provision of rock shelters protecting the nests and the sitting birds from the elements. Normally the duck is allowed to lay a full clutch of eggs before the down crop is taken, and a proportion of down – usually that in poorer condition in the bottom of the nest – is left as a basis for a further crop which the sitting bird plucks from her breast. The first crop is usually the best but it has been found that two, or even three collections can be made, eider down even of poor quality being superior to any other insulating material for quilts and similar articles. In Labrador, where a third collection has been more common, it has been found that the sitting bird would use vegetation as a substitute without a noticeable diminution in hatching success.

The protection of eiders goes back much further than the eider down industry, probably beginning in the 7th century with St.

European eider drake wing-stretching, showing the full wing pattern

Cuthbert's sojourn on the Farne Islands off the Northumberland coast. Since that time the eiders of the Farnes seem to have been regarded with considerable affection by the local population, and are still familiarly known as "cuddy ducks".

If we look at colloquial names for eiders in various parts of the world we are almost overwhelmed with information. I will simply refer to some of the English and Eskimo names known to me. In North America the terms sea ducks and sea drakes have a wide usage. Local terms illustrate how they can confuse the broader issue of correct naming of birds. For example the terms sea-coot and black-and-white coot are locally used, both for this species and for scoters – another small group of marine diving ducks. But neither eiders nor scoters are closely related to the coots proper, which belong to the family of rails, Rallidae. The name canvas-back is also locally used and can also cause confusion, for the canvas-back proper is a fresh-water diving duck of the pochard tribe Aythyini. Other local names in North America include wamp, pied wamp, shoal duck, squam duck, squaw duck (confusing eider with old-squaw – a different species of sea duck), laying duck, looby, and Eskimo duck.

North American Eskimo names for the eider also vary from region to region but are all basically similar including Miteg, Meet-tirk, Mitirk, Mittivik, Metik and Mittek. My Eskimo friend

A pair of American eiders in flight

Noah in the Belcher Islands called me Mitirk after seeing me with my eider ducklings. It is interesting that the Eskimos, living as they do in close association with their prey animals, have different names for the sexes of many species, just as we have different gender names for our domestic animals, such as dog and bitch, bull and cow, buck and doe, ram and ewe, and boar and sow. For example, in Baffin Island the eiders generally are known as Metik or Mittek, but Amaulik is also used for the male and Arnaviak for the female. Similar variations apply elsewhere in the North American arctic, and doubtless in other arctic regions also.

Eiders of both sexes are fairly easy to distinguish in the field, the male with its black flanks, belly and tail contrasting noticeably with the predominant white of the rest of the plumage. Under certain conditions the black on the male's crown may also be seen. At close quarters the female can be identified from other species by the close black barring on the brown feathers. At a distance the large size, with long yet chunky body and elongated head profile, are distinctive in both sexes, particularly in flight. The flight is unusual amongst ducks in that it normally consists of alternate series of wing-beats and glides, usually low over the water, and groups commonly fly in single file. A further distinctive feature of the male in flight is the white fore-wing which contrasts with the black flight feathers.

As in other duck species the drake eider moults into an "eclipse" plumage after the breeding season, starting around the beginning of July and lasting until November or December. In eclipse the plumage is mostly black except for the wing patch; this shows as a white flash on the sides when the wings are folded. Drake eiders take 3 to 4 years to acquire their full plumage. During their first winter and spring the basically female-type plumage becomes darker on the head, and over the whole of the plumage development period the white areas of the full male plumage are gradually developed and the brown areas which are left become darker until the full black and white breeding dress is acquired. This mongrel-type plumage of immature drake eiders, and the eclipse plumage of adult males, result in a bewildering variety of dark and light plumage patterns, but the basic shape of the bird is always distinctive.

Taking the different populations of the North American common eiders as a whole, the species may be regarded as a partial migrant for, as we have seen, some birds stay in the arctic all year round. In those groups which do migrate south for the winter, including the northern eiders we worked with in Labrador, the northward migration back to the breeding grounds begins around the end of March and the beginning of April. The northern eiders that winter off the New England coasts gather on sandbars before leaving, and then the males go first. But the females and immatures must catch up with them at some point for they arrive in Labrador in mixed flocks of varying numbers up to a hundred birds or more. The southernmost breeding areas begin to be occupied in mid-May, though the more northerly populations are not established until well into June. Courtship displays may be seen before, during, and after the migratory movements, and nesting begins almost immediately. There is no time to waste, for the arctic summer is a very short one. In June a large proportion of the adult males leave the breeding colonies to gather in flocks, this coinciding with the beginning of their eclipse moult. Some males are on the move southwards in late summer, but the main exodus begins in October, the young by now of course being fully-winged. By mid-December the migratory populations have reached their winter quarters along the Atlantic coast of the U.S.A. as far north as Massachusetts as long as there is open water. The general winter conditions for these birds are probably not much less severe than they are for those birds which stay in the open leads of Hudson Bay. The arctic air temperature may be lower but the more southerly birds have rough surf to contend with. All the subspecies of common eider in North America, and the majority of the eiders of the Old World, show remarkably efficient adaptations to aquatic living in arctic climates. Only the penguins of the Antarctic surpass them in this respect.

4 On Being a Female Eider

"The souls of little children are marvellously delicate and tender things, and keep for ever the shadow that first falls on them." Olive Schreiner.

They say that children are a blessing, and it is as well that this should be so, but anyone who has been regarded by a brood of ducklings as their mother will consider them a blessing that is rather mixed. If I had known, on that fateful day in the tundra when I picked up a hatching eider egg and took it home as the beginning of a family – if I had known the consequences I might have recoiled in horror. For when a duckling hatches, it becomes psychologically fixed upon the most suitable parent-object in its environment. Normally, in the case of eider ducklings, this is an eider duck, but in the case of my brood it was me. It was me they regarded as mother, it was I who became the object of their anatine affections, the ideal eider. And as far as they were concerned – "once a duck, always a duck!" The consquences can only partly be imagined.

The role of ducks' mother was in fact forced upon me by circumstances. In that first, fateful tundra summer Nic and I were faced with a serious problem: no research material. For the expedition had been mounted to study the display behaviour of adult, breeding eider ducks. And there weren't any. I had consulted ornithologists who knew that part of the world, considered the breeding requirements of eiders, studied the maps for likely nesting areas, and decided upon the estuary of False River where it flows north into Ungava Bay near the northern tip of Quebec Labrador. This is one of the more accessible areas of the Canadian sub-arctic where eiders breed, and one of the most southerly. Thus we should have a good chance of finding breeding eiders fairly easily – we would be able to get there without too much difficulty, and the break-up of the ice would come early. And there was the added advantage that the area had been visited by several other biologists from the University, and the logistics of transport and so on were well known.

So after a hectic period of preparation during which plans were made, modified, re-arranged, and finalised, we felt full of hope. We had cut down our equipment to the minimum consistent with safety. We didn't have an enormous burden of food to take with us for we were confident of living off the land to a certain extent. And we weren't going to be far from civilisation anyway. So off we went, thrown around inside a battered old Dakota like gravel inside a lobster shell, landing at Fort Chimo near the estuary of False River. The break-up of the ice was not in fact complete and there was a lot of pack ice still floating down the rivers, so we couldn't use boat transport. And at that slushy time of the year travelling by dog team is not really feasible. But after a week of waiting the water was clear enough for us to persuade an Eskimo with a serviceable boat to take us and our gear round into False River. It was now the first week in June. Three months later everything would be freezing up again.

I froze up almost immediately. As my research grant was not sufficient to cover proper arctic clothing I was trying to make do with English winter clothing worn in several layers. But it just wasn't the same as the proper Eskimo gear we acquired later. In the bottom of that boat, trying to get some sleep with just the floor boards between me and the ice water, I was colder than I have ever been before or since.

But we did find somewhere to establish our base camp, as planned. It took us a couple of days to sort ourselves out – to get used to the gigantic scale of things in the tundra. It is a kind of horizontal enormousness. The river was like a lake, the lakes like seas, and the tundra a mixture of rock, water, and bog stretching to the horizon in all directions. But after two days of reorientation, and with the help of our Eskimo friends, we established our camp and were based there for the rest of the season.

As soon as we had made camp and settled ourselves a bit – and this takes a day or two when you are living in isolation and have to be ready for anything – we began to scour the area for study material. We had naturally been keeping our eyes skinned for any sign of eiders since we arrived in the north. There were quite a few about as we sailed round into the river; not as many as we would like, but they were there. My forecast seemed to have been correct. But when we came to look for signs of adult eiders performing their complex and beautiful mating displays we were completely frustrated. Because there weren't any. We would see the odd eider flying by from time to time, and occasionally hear the crooning of the drakes, but we didn't find a single pair, let alone watch them displaying.

We searched far and wide but eiders came there none. Days went by, then weeks, and it became obvious that though the eiders may have achieved their ends we weren't going to achieve ours. We discovered later that the area had been shot over by a party of hunters shortly before we arrived, and any drakes that were still around had been scared away. We knew it was nearing the end of the display season, for that begins in the fall and ends in the spring when the females take to their nests and don't like to be bothered any more. And in the tundra they make their nests at the earliest possibility, for the summer is so short they have to be quickly on the job in order to allow the ducklings time to reach the flying stage before the freeze-up. But there should have been enough display to study. After all, one can only concentrate on one mating at a time.

But it was no use. We had to admit defeat. And so we were faced with a very tricky decision. We couldn't leave the area for we were funded by an Arctic Research Scholarship and Field Grant that required me to carry out arctic research towards my doctorate. We therefore had to find another research project of such a nature that I would be able to make "an original contribution to science" as required for a Doctorate of Philosophy, the usual research degree. So what to do? That was a very stressful time. I studied as much display in other species of birds as I could. We documented the lives of a colony of spiders, as mentioned in Chapter 2. And we set up an elegant little study of the rate of decay of carcasses under various conditions. But none of these things, I knew, was likely to produce results worthy of a doctorate. Camp was disgruntled and smelly.

On July the 7th, almost exactly a month after we had set up camp, we were exploring the islands in the river, seeking research material and also edible protein, in company with another pair of biologists visiting the area who had a big, powered canoe. For various reasons we hadn't visited the islands before, largely because they were several miles away and rather difficult to get to. We landed on three of the islands, un-named on the map and christened by me after three excellent field biologists, all friends and ex-pupils of mine: Humph, Middy, and Bladder. David Humphries, John Midwinter, and Bladder Hansen (so-called because of frequent necessary interludes when he is in the field).

On each of the islands there were sizeable colonies of nesting eiders, sitting tight on well-incubated eggs. So it was a good area for eiders after all. And here was excellent research material: ducklings. Ducklings to imprint, to experiment with, to study in all sorts of ways. Modesty has never been one of my strong points and I felt that if Konrad Lorenz could imprint mallard ducklings to himself, I could imprint eiders. Lorenz did his work while living at home, with his mallards in semi-captivity and my task would be more difficult. But I knew that no one had yet imprinted any bird to themselves in the field, under natural conditions except for the parent substitution. I decided to try. What a portentous decision that was! So much was to arise from it of wonder and despair, of frustration and achievement. My notes say simply "July 7. Eider juvenile no.1, obtained 2100 hrs. Bladder Island, nest with 2 young, 1 egg, and 'E.1' hatching. I assisted emergence and kept covered until the 8th." A dozen eider hatchings later, the notes covering the same happening and period of time would have occupied many pages of my notebook, with drawings on hatching movements, shell breakage, and duckling behaviour, with notes on all these things and on comparisons with other individuals, and with an additional photographic record.

From the islands we took a selection of other eggs which we judged to be near to hatching, for one experimental animal was not going to be enough for any valid conclusions to be drawn, although papers are published in the psychological literature based upon observations on one individual. In ethology we try to obtain data from 20 randomly-selected individuals of the same species. This, as J.B.S. Haldane pointed out, is enough for statistical validity of the evidence. If 20 randomly selected animals all show the same response to the same stimulus or circumstances, then the likelihood that this is other than basic in the behavioural repertoire of the animal is very small indeed. By the end of the second season I had had 20 randomly selected ducklings through my hands, in all senses of the phrase, and had made confirmatory observations on hundreds of others living under natural conditions in the same area at the same time. I believe I can be sure of my data. Always allowing of course for personal bias in observation. It is difficult to see everything, to avoid favouring some subjectively more interesting part of the behavioural spectrum spread before you.

In animal behaviour studies, as in any other scientific endeavour, continuous concentration and application are as important as objectivity. For usually one needs a continuous record, at least in naturalistic studies in the field and preferably in laboratory studies also, because what an animal does before and after an experiment may have an important bearing on the data generated by the experiment. In my case this need for continuous observation of the egg or duckling in hand was of particular importance, for I had decided to study the natural development of the ducklings' behaviour from before hatching until they were able to look after themselves. To this end I would not only, effectively, need to become a duck, I would also have to keep watch for as many hours of the day and night as possible. Fortunately, I had an assistant of enormous strength and perseverance who was able to take on his broad shoulders all the everyday camp chores and other non-scientific tasks so that I could be freed for almost continuous observation.

For about three days before a duckling hatches — the same as in chickens — the bird's behaviour inside the egg can be observed by cutting a little hole in the "blunt" end so that one can see into the air space where the bird's head is resting. Thus one can see hatching movements and hear what the bird is saying, as detailed in the next chapter. Then for about a week after hatching the bird is developing its basic adaptations to its environment. It comes into the world equipped with a spectrum of abilities, some operative almost from the time of hatching, others gradually developing as it gains experience of its environment. Unless one observes as much as possible of the total spectrum of behaviour — the total transactional complex — one is likely to miss something of crucial importance, such as the first instance of a particular reaction, or the infrequent occurrence of a rarely-used piece of instinctive behaviour.

While eggs were hatching therefore, I had to make careful observations as frequently as possible. I decided upon four-hourly observations day and night. This was not as bad as it sounds, for I was incubating the eggs in my tent and all I had to do was flutter awake, roll over, and see what was what. Sometimes there was nothing and I could go back to sleep having recorded the fact. At other times of course all sorts of things would be happening, and, as many of the eggs were at the same stage of development, a number would frequently be hatching at the same time, which made life difficult. But too much data is better than too little. And the hatchings were fairly soon over and I could get a good night's rest.

Of course, after the first eggs hatched I had ducklings to deal with as well as eggs, and was required to be out and about leading the brood around from pond to pond so that they could develop their natural feeding mechanisms and obtain enough nourishment. At the same time their every movement was being religiously recorded. In this way I spent around 200 hours in or at the edges of tundra pools or the sea with my brood, with rare trips out onto the open water, my family following faithfully. To them I was a female eider. And from time to time I began to think so myself. I spoke eiderese – it is a simple language, as I explain later, and

The author and brood of ducklings, Belcher Islands, Hudson Bay

quickly learned – and I would converse with my brood as we went about our normal anatine affairs. I would find myself choosing a good place to feed, or rest, without consciously thinking about it. My movements became subdued automatically in order to avoid distressing the children. It was as if I was walking on the moon and needed to reduce my movements in order to avoid taking off. I had to wade slowly and quietly through the water; otherwise I would cause a great swirl and the ducklings would dive, reacting as if they had been attacked.

As with any other children, the propinquity of my brood was occasionally to be regretted. If one is recording the doings of a well-imprinted bird in one's notebook and that bird reaches up and tweaks the pencil out of one's hand one is inclined to give it a clout where it should have its ears. One can't do that of course so it is all a little frustrating. But one can swear at ducklings – quietly – for they don't understand our language (though I occasionally had my suspicions!), and it can be quite an amusing experience to have a duckling performing – sometimes literally of course – on one's lap, knees, or head, while one is calling it all the names under the tundra sun. But if I had known that I could not leave a 2-day old imprinted duckling without it crying for me, or that I would have to give them 8 hours a day in the water so that they could catch enough food, I might have thought twice about taking on the job.

The job of being a duck's mother, it must be admitted, did have its compensations, apart from the intellectual excitement of the scientific discoveries. On one occasion, for example, when I was in a pond with my brood an adult female eider duck flew over, circled round obviously attracted by the ducklings, and dropped down to land smoothly on the pond. The ducklings had never seen anything like this before. Nothing like the mother they had grown to know so closely. With calls of distress they came rushing back across the water to where I was standing in the shallows, their cries changing to contentment calls as they reached me, and producing a positive profusion of head-toss greetings. The adult eider thus had me brought to her attention and departed in haste, and doubtless with her bird brain in a state of simple confusion.

I think my proudest moment was late in our second arctic summer when we were on the shores of the Belcher Islands in Hudson Bay. I had two broods at the time, one older than the other. The older brood was really adolescent and beginning to show a considerable degree of independence. So much so that they would occasionally have to be driven to shore in the evening by

someone who had had to launch the boat especially. And they would perform the usual greeting ceremonies but not come when they were called.

One fine day I decided to take this older brood out onto the water. They enjoyed following the kayak and I found it stimulating to be treated as an eider on the water as well as on the land. So I set off with my ducklings swimming and diving around me, paddling gently towards the research vessel *Calanus* which happened to be visiting the area. At a point on the shore opposite the boat the ducklings seemed to find an especially interesting source of food, and stayed there diving vigorously even though I moved on and called them quietly to follow. So I thought I would paddle over to the boat and see some human friends for a change, which I did. "Hi!" said a bearded figure in the dinghy at the stern, "where's the ducklings?"

"Over there" I said, waving casually towards the shore several hundred yards away, and hoping desperately that he was not going to do what he obviously was going to.

"Well – fetch 'em over!" he said.

I had to try. I had my British face to save. So I called in best eiderese across the water: the low, rather hoarse cohesion call of the adult female eider – "cow-cow-cow. How-cow-cow-cow". The ducklings' necks stretched up in the alarm posture. They had only just realised I was so far away! But would they come? Not only would they have to swim across a large stretch of water in order to join me, they would have to swim towards a large unfamiliar object which they weren't to know was the harmless *Calanus.*

I called again, and slowly, but with increasing confidence, they came swimming across, giving the upward nod of greeting most of the way, right up to the kayak.

Before I had ducklings to imprint I had to have successful incubation techniques. And remember, we were not equipped to work with ducklings or eggs. We were expecting only to be observing adults. So we had to produce a make-shift incubator which would do the job, with care, as well as the mother duck herself. For the ducklings would have to be normal on hatching, otherwise I would not be able to say that my observations were valid. Fortunately I had kept ducks and reared ducklings before, and I knew eiders pretty well at all stages from my early primitive work at the Wildfowl Trust.

We found that a cardboard box lined with eiderdown and covered with woollen clothing, warmed with polythene bottles of hot water, would keep the necessary temperature for a few hours. But there remained the problem of humidity. Eggs must be in a humid atmosphere to develop properly. If the humidity is too low they lose too much moisture and have difficulties with hatching even if they survive that long. And water birds seem to require a higher humidity than other species. We quickly found the ideal solution – a super-saturated solution of woolly sock! With a wet sock around the hot water bottles the incubator atmosphere was maintained at an appropriate level of humidity. It must have been appropriate, for quite a few successful hatchings resulted.

My friend Middy actually made me a portable incubator for our second season's work in the north, with a paraffin-burning wick as heating element and a bi-metallic strip as the thermostat. But we found that the 35 degree daily range of ambient temperature was too much for the incubator to cope with, and the fumes were something of a problem in an enclosed space. So we fell back on the wet sock and hot water bottle technique. The hot water had to be renewed every four hours, but as I had to make observations at that frequency anyway it didn't matter too much. Except to Nic who had to heat the water. Sometimes the system would break down of course due to us trying to do too much at the same time. I then retired to my sleeping bag with eggs, or ducklings, and kept them warm by suitable placement under the arms or in the crutch. It was a little tricky because of the possibility of squashing the poor things, but I am pleased to say I had no fatalities in that way.

Later, I found that the ducklings actually preferred to be

cuddled when they were resting – unless the weather was very warm. As I walked around the tundra from pond to pond I would sometimes pick the ducklings up and put them in my hunting bag or in my parka, particularly if I was in a hurry. They would settle quite comfortably, given a suitable place to nestle, and I began to suspect that they must show an equivalent behaviour in the natural state. Sure enough, eventually I saw ducklings being carried on the parent's back, and later on again found references to this in the biological literature.

Living with one's animals in this way makes it possible to understand them as natural units. And I am sure that it enables one to see things which would escape the casual observer or the laboratory experimenter. For example, in our second season I was walking slowly through a pond with a brood a few days old, when a long-tailed duck, or "old-squaw", flew in and landed on the pond. It seemed that she had been attracted by the ducklings, for she swam to and fro showing great interest in our end of the pond. And I was sure she wouldn't stay there in my presence otherwise. So I watched her very carefully, forgetting about my brood swimming close by. Then she took off with the old-squaw alarm call and departed at speed.

When I returned my attention to my charges, they had disappeared! They weren't in view anywhere. I assumed, momentarily, that by chance they must be all under water at the same time. So I waited for them to surface. But they didn't. For a few seconds I was thoroughly confused. And then I found them sitting quietly, as David's drawing (overleaf) so nicely shows, bunched in my "danger shadow", hiding from trouble.

This danger reaction of hiding behind the parent is quite innate; an inborn automatic response to certain specific stimuli. I had seen that this was the ducklings' response to an alarm-calling parent. Whether it is also the response to the presence of a predator without the alarm call being given I was unable to discover. But it is always a response to something very definite and specific. My ducklings were showing a good example of instinctive behaviour. But as a reaction to what? They didn't hide as soon as the old-squaw landed. They hid on her departure. So it looks as if they were responding to *her* alarm call by hiding behind *me:* which is interesting enough. But it is also possible that there was some kind of visual signal given during her departure which produced the response. Certainly, my ear cannot detect any real similarity between the alarm calls of eider and old-squaw. The eider's is a throaty, descending, rattling whirr, and the old-squaw's is a rising,

simple, two-note yodel. Anyway, the point is that if I had not been playing the part of a female eider in the natural environment we would probably never have known that this problem exists.

The female eider's alarm whirr was a very useful means of getting the ducklings to return to me in a hurry. If the mother gives the cohesion call consistently the brood will close up somewhat, but the natural function of this call is not to get the ducklings to come to mother, only to keep fairly close so that they don't get lost. On the alarm whirr, however, they come running – or steaming across the water, to sit quietly behind the female. Thus, when I wanted to go back to camp having decided that the observations were concluded for the present all I had to do was give the alarm whirr once and when they were settled in my danger shadow pick the ducklings quietly up and put them in my bag or parka. Or else I would walk out of the pond, calling gently, and the ducklings would slowly follow. Then we would preen ourselves for a while on the bank, they in their way, me in mine, before going home.

If I was in a hurry to get home I would pick the ducklings up. But on many occasions I would walk the tundra with the ducklings in tow. As Konrad Lorenz pointed out in the case of his mallard ducklings, the brood follows at a distance consistent with the height of the natural parent. Thus, if I lay down and crawled – which was seldom, because it is not really convenient in the tundra – they would stay in very close contact; almost touching. If I crawled on all fours they would follow at a slightly greater distance. And if I walked along normally they would follow at a greater distance still. To the ducklings the natural parent should be a certain height, and if the parent substitute is the wrong height they adjust it, as it were, by staying at an appropriate distance where the height *looks* right. The only occasions when the ducklings followed very close when I was standing was when they came close accidentally and then followed my boots, each of which was approximately the size of a rather large duck. Incidentally, I never began to develop webbed feet! This was the arctic, remember, and I had to wear thigh boots and several layers of socks.

This close approach when I lay down was a delight in some ways but a damned nuisance in others. My "mother and child" photographs show how close that degree of togetherness could be. And it was annoying when one lay down to get a duck's eye view of the brood for a photograph to have the ducklings walk up with the apparent intention of registering themselves, rather than their image, on the sensitive film.

Imprinted duckling nestling contentedly between the author's shins whilst he is lying down

The consistency with which my imprinted ducklings followed me was well-nigh incredible. They seemed to have been as well-imprinted to me as they would have been to their natural mother. They would follow, over any terrain, and even if I walked over jagged rocks, to put them on their mettle, they would follow, albeit with hesitations and complaints. But normally they came with me everywhere, producing a continuous chorus of cohesion calls.

Only once did a young brood of ducklings temporarily desert me, and that was for a very good reason. One day when the brood

had cleaned up all the available food animals in a small pond I refused to go on to another pond as was our custom. The result was fascinating. To begin with the ducklings simply walked out on to the land and preened themselves dry as usual. They they began to be restless. They obviously didn't want to return to the water. They were hungry, and in normal circumstances the mother would have moved on to another pool where there was more food. They walked around fussily, sat down again, slipped in and out of the water, and gradually began to wander away short distances in an increasingly "well, let's get on with it" sort of way. But I stayed put. I wanted to see what would happen. Eventually, after much to-ing and fro-ing, the whole brood walked away across the tundra, complaining as they went: a remarkable example of apparently human and intelligent behaviour, but entirely governed by instinctive drives. They were hungry and so had to find other food. They were imprinted to me and so needed to stay in my company. Hunger eventually won and they moved away, giving the complaint calls which are usual when the distance between them and mother is increasing uncomfortably.

A knowledge of the innate language of eider ducklings – my discovery and description of which is detailed in chapter 6 – was of use to me in a number of ways. Each of the six vocal signals meant something very specific, from contentment to distress, and in this way I knew more or less what the ducklings were doing without having to keep them in view. The distress call was not high on our list of signals because it is given when the duckling is in real danger, and this seldom happened with my brood. One day, however, Nic and I were consuming a well-earned meal in our tent by the waters of Hudson Bay when a positive chorus of distress calls burst forth close at hand. I rushed out of the tent to find, to my amazement, a small brood of ducklings – mine – being

attacked by a gull in the shallow water. I had left the ducklings in their box in my tent while re-fuelling, but somehow they had escaped and wandered into the sea. Fortunately, when they began to suffer the natural consequences of going off on their own, their innate distress calls, and our knowledge of them, enabled me to effect a rescue.

The variety of innate behaviours was much greater than I had expected when I first started working with the ducklings, but even more unexpected was the ability with which the birds would cope with new situations. On the 27th of July for example I was out with E.3, then five days old and having its tenth outing in the big wide world. My notes read as follows: "Diving beautifully. Taking food under water very easily now and swimming around beneath the surface most proficiently. At the end of the feeding session the bird emerged from the pool and came to preen by me by a very difficult detour which it took with no hesitation. This involved taking a roundabout route so that it could reach my position which was on the usual rock – a miniature cliff to the bird – approximately 4 ft above the surface of the pool and which could only be reached by a circuitous route. Taking this route involved climbing a steep slope through dwarf birch, during which time I was completely hidden from the bird because it had to go behind the end of the rock. There was a certain amount of distress calling but not nearly so insistent as in real danger or emergency."

Less expected still, and even more exciting, was this instance taken from my notes on July 18th the next year when I was out with three five-day old ducklings on their 21st trip: "The three ducklings dived for food immediately when placed in water. 1050 hrs a strange eider duckling appeared on the other side of the pond about 20 yards away. I gave the 'cow-cow-cow-cow' call of the female and it came all the way across the pond to the water's edge, producing the distress call without ceasing. Its homing on the sound of my call was very definite; there is no doubt at all that the call was that to which the strange duckling was attracted. When I stopped calling after it reached the water's edge, my own ducklings re-entered the water whence they had emerged when I called and the stranger stayed with them. Only then did it cease its distress call. The stranger gave the full greeting (cohesion call plus upward nod) to my ducklings but was very apprehensive of them. At the same time three female old-squaws had flown into the pond, and for some minutes they were all swimming together about 15 feet from me. 1058 hrs. the old-squaws flew off; they had shown great interest in the ducklings all the time they were present. Also 1058 my ducklings emerged to preen near me, showing the worrying-of-moss-etc. behaviour, with contentment notes. 1059 hrs. the stranger emerged also but only to the water's edge, producing occasional distress calls. 1100 hrs. my ducklings re-entered water and continued diving. The stranger would not dive, swimming with the others on the surface and intermittently giving the distress call; my ducklings not afraid of it at all. When the stranger was first approaching me it gave the query-alert call once. My ducklings give the full greeting to the stranger as well as to each other. 1106 hrs. the stranger gave the distress call from some distance away; I called and it came towards the sound, still giving the distress call. This induced the other ducklings to follow at high speed (following a distress-calling fellow moving towards the parent). 1108 hrs. the stranger first properly emerged to sit with the others while they preened. It relaxed a little and occasionally almost closed its eyes or took a little interest in potential food-objects. 1110 hrs. all re-entered water. Definite greetings being given to stranger with no response. When others all diving, stranger still giving distress call. 1112 hrs. stranger looked beneath water twice in typical fashion and then dived, continuing to do so, but still very apprehensive. Diving mechanism exactly the same as in the others. 1115 hrs. all emerged about 20 feet from me. When I approached, stranger re-entered water but stayed within 6 to 8 feet, diving. 1119 hrs. stranger emerged to sit with others at my feet, me crouching motionless, the birds about 2 feet away, all in an irregularity of the rock surface. 1120 hrs. they all re-entered water. 1125 hrs. I sat on low rock at water level and they all came to feed round my feet, then passing by me to re-enter water. Stranger chasing mosquitoes in exactly the same way as the others. 1130 hrs. herring gull approached; I gave the alarm whirr and they all collected at water's edge and emerged to stay quietly at my feet. Stranger more noticeably alarmed at the gull than were the others. 1138, I picked them all up after they had emerged again after more feeding. Stranger allowed my slow gentle approach as did the others. It reacted very positively to brooding contact, thrusting its head firmly between my fingers when I enclosed it in my hand. Carried them back to camp in the hood of my parka, which provides warmth, darkness, and some pressure. All were quiet."

This extract shows how close a relationship I was able to develop with ducklings only a few days old. It also shows how I was able to induce a strange duckling, about the same age as the others, to join with my brood in the absence of its natural mother. But it did not develop any real association with me, presumably because it was imprinted to a female eider. Later, when I changed the ducklings over to artificial food, the stranger refused to feed and died after 15 days with the brood. This was very sad, but it would have died anyway if left to its own devices. Sooner or later, probably sooner, a predator would have taken it, for the mother duck's principal role, apart from that of a mobile brooder, is to protect the ducklings from predatory attack.

This account of the different behaviour of the stranger indicates an extreme case of a difference in "personality" between ducklings. Another example is given by the behaviour of a whole brood of 5 strangers who appeared with their mother in my pool one day. On the same pool there was also a brood of 7 old-squaw ducklings which had lost their mother, in addition to my two broods of 4 ducklings each: a superb situation for opportunistic natural experiments and comparative observations. It was easy to tell which the strangers were for they carried their heads on upstretched necks in the alert posture, and showed other indications of apprehensiveness only noticeable to someone who knew what their natural behaviour would have been if I had been their mother. They were very much interested in joining my ducklings and showed a definite tendency to come to my call, but the sight of me was too much for them. One of them, however, was much less fearful than the others and approached to mingle with my birds a number of times. Eventually I was able to pick it up while it was preening without it being greatly distressed. Such a difference in behaviour in the case of a human child would, I think, be regarded as indicating a difference in personality.

In the case of my own birds the difference between individuals was more noticeable, though only to me of course because I was the only one who knew them intimately. Except in the case of one bird – he could be recognised by anyone I pointed him out to because he had a slightly different profile from the others. Birds don't have a face, as we know it, expressing themselves instead by plumage, vocalisations, and movements. But this bird certainly had a different head shape from the others, and different behaviour too. He tended to lag behind, both in the water and on land. Perhaps his brain was slightly different from the others', as a result of the different skull shape. Indeed, it may be that a similar structural difference in humans is responsible for certain differences in personality. But the problem of the definition of personality is a very complex one, exercising the minds of numerous psychologists without much meaningful result from the point of view of the behavioural biologist. Suffice it to say that I could tell my ducklings apart whether I could see the coloured rings on their legs or not.

I could fill the whole book with accounts of the joys and tribulations of being a female eider. But a more formalised

approach will probably be better and in the next two chapters I give an account of hatching behaviour and of the duckling's development in the natural environment.

5 The Hazards of Hatching

The history of a bird's egg, from its formation in the ovary of the female to the emergence from the shell of the fully-developed embryo, is a fascinating story of biological ingenuity. The bird's egg, like those of insects and reptiles, is laid on land and protected by the surrounding embryonic membranes and shell. It is more or less a self-contained system, the embryo feeding on the store of yolk, protected from dessication by its membranes, breathing by a network of blood vessels which transport the oxygen absorbed through the pores of the shell, and mechanically protected by the strong, calcareous shell. But this system has its drawbacks: for example what does one do with the excretory waste products of metabolism? Mechanically, this problem is not too difficult to solve, for the excretory products simply accumulate in a special sac which is left behind when the embryo leaves the shell. But most of the nitrogenous waste products of metabolism, such as urea, are poisonous. If birds excreted urea, as mammals do, they would poison themselves in the egg, for the urea would circulate in the blood stream, being soluble in water. Instead, birds excrete uric acid, which is insoluble in water and therefore stays more or less inert in the excretory sac.

The egg proper is the single female egg cell, or ovum, which is shed from the ovary. Like all other eggs this is enclosed in a vitelline membrane, the basic, primary, protective membrane of the cell. Some animals, like insects, have a secondary membrane formed by special cells in the ovary, which hardens to form the shell. Additionally, tertiary structures may be formed in the oviduct or by accessory glands. Avian tertiary products include the albumen, or white of the egg, the membranes lining the shell, and the shell itself. The bird's ovum is fertilized, of course, before these tertiary structures are added. After fertilization, as the egg passes down the oviduct, it first receives the albumen, then the two shell membranes, and finally the shell itself which, like the albumen, is deposited in layers. Pigments are secreted as the layering of the shell is taking place, and finally a thin cuticle is deposited over the shell, also pigmented, to give the shell colouration typical of the species.

The eggs of eiders, as is well known, are laid in nests plentifully supplied with down. This material has very high insulating properties, hence its commercial use in a variety of insulating manufactured articles such as eiderdowns. The down is obtained by the female plucking it from her own breast. This also makes a brood patch on her underside where the feathering has become sparse and the heat of her body can pass more easily to the eggs. Many birds develop brood spots by a special restricted moult of feathers, but waterbirds need to maintain better insulation than moulting would allow.

The necessary conditions of temperature, humidity and mechanical protection for incubation to proceed satisfactorily are of course provided by the sitting bird. The period of incubation is usually regarded as the time which elapses from the completion of the clutch to the hatching of the brood. But several groups of birds begin incubation with the laying of the first egg; these include the pelicans, parrots, hummingbirds and many birds of prey. The result is that the eggs do not hatch together and the young therefore are of different sizes. This would seem to be an adaptation to occasional restrictions in food supply. If food is short the younger and weaker nestlings are at a distinct disadvantage in the competition for what the parents bring to the nest, and may die. However, the older young normally survive these conditions which they might not do if the food was shared out equally.

The eider begins incubation upon completion of the clutch of around 5 eggs, and it takes around 30 days for the eggs to hatch. The length of the incubation period in birds has been a matter of considerable dispute and confusion for some time. Aristotle assumed that the length of the incubation period was dependent upon the size of the egg and gave a number of incorrect incubation periods which were copied for 2,000 years. We now know that the proper period for the satisfactory development of the embryo depends on a number of complex interacting factors and is not directly dependent on the size of the egg. The range of avian incubation periods is from about 80 days in the royal albatross to 10 days in the smallest perching birds. When eggs are placed in artificial incubators it is impossible to reduce the natural period of incubation by more than one day. This suggests that the natural incubation programme is working at optimal efficiency.

The incubation temperature – about 38 degrees C in eiders and other ducks — is maintained by the sitting bird within remarkably narrow limits. The eggs are warmed by the brood patch on the breast and belly of the parent, and covered by the mantle of feathers which the sitting bird arranges around them. In cold weather the incubating bird sits tighter, and in very hot weather she may rise off the eggs and shade them with her wings. The efficiency of the parental control of egg temperature may be seen in the case of the emperor penguin which breeds in the antarctic winter in temperatures as low as −78 degrees C, in bitterly cold winds. The temperature of the single egg, supported on the feet and covered with an abdominal fold of feathered skin is maintained at around 34 degrees C for 53 days. At the other extreme, a nighthawk nesting on a flat roof is known to be able to keep the temperature of its eggs down to 64 degrees C when the roof temperature exceeds 78 degrees C.

An incubating eider may not leave the next for days on end, sitting tight for most of that time. But she cannot sit without moving because the eggs need to be turned from time to time. The difference in temperature between the part of the eggs in contact with the bird's body and the underside of the eggs next to the ground may be considerable. Also, if the eggs are not turned the embryos may adhere to the membranes lining the shell and would not be able to develop properly. In the natural state eggs are turned very frequently, sometimes as often as once an hour. This occurs when the incubating bird stands up to stretch herself or to move into a more comfortable position on the eggs. Also, of course, when she leaves the nest to defaecate or drink. Little food is taken while eiders are incubating. The eggs are rearranged in the nest by the bird moving them accidentally with the feet or deliberately with the bill, and the result is a random turning, and even a shifting in the relative positions of the eggs in the clutch.

Eggs of the domestic fowl in artificial incubators may be turned as often as every 15 minutes with increasing hatching success, and they should be turned at least 5 times in 24 hours, in alternate directions. If they are not turned atall only 15 percent will hatch. Towards the end of the incubation period the sitting bird sits much tighter and turns the eggs less, and it has been found that leaving eggs in artificial incubators unturned for the last few days before hatching does not reduce the hatching success. It may even increase it, the reason for which we may see later.

Only the female eider incubates, the sharing of incubation duties being a very variable habit in different birds according to their particular adaptations. Drake eiders are very brightly coloured and would attract the attention of potential predators to the nest if they were to incubate. The female eider being very well camouflaged is difficult to see on the nest, particularly when she crouches and remains motionless – which is what she does if an intruder appears. Only when a potential predator comes very close does the sitting bird leave the nest. This she then does in a clamour and commotion, often defaecating over the eggs and apparently making the maximum amount of noise in order to lure the predator away.

I have given this background to the biology of incubation in the eider to show how important it is for the incubating bird to perform the correct activities if the brood is to survive. The behaviour of the incubating bird involves instinctive acts developed as a result of natural selection and genetically incorporated into the basic make-up of the species.

My tasks in hatching my ducklings was much easier that that of the female eider, for I obtained my eggs by selecting those which were within a few days of hatching. The turning of my eggs was therefore not a critical matter, and the maintenance of the correct conditions of temperature and humidity covered a relatively short period of time.

It is not difficult to tell when an egg is near to the time of hatching, because 2 to 3 days before the hatching process begins the duckling's bill pierces the inner shell membrane and protrudes into the air space in the blunt end of the egg. Typically, the two membranes which line the shell separate at the blunt end of the egg to form an air space. This increases in volume as the embryo develops, and when the embryo has become a duckling ready to emerge into the big wide world the air space has reached its maximum volume, principally by the absorption of air through the shell.

When the duckling's bill pierces the membrane into the air space, it begins to breathe air, using its lungs for the first time. From this point on one can hear sounds from inside the shell, for the duckling begins to vocalise and also to produce the "clicking" sound – often called tapping – associated with hatching. Thus, if an egg is making noises – and one can detect these easily enough even in an intact egg by cupping the hands around it against the ear – one knows it is near to hatching. So in most cases I didn't have long to wait for my eggs to hatch.

The author listening for sounds from a duckling inside an egg at a nesting site in Belcher Islands, Hudson Bay

Now, as I had several eggs hatching or about to hatch, it seemed obvious that here was a golden opportunity to make a complete study of all the behavioural factors associated with the hatching process, and also to see if anything the duckling was doing inside the egg had any significance in relation to what it did after it emerged. But this turned out to be a more complex matter than I had bargained for. The pattern of shell cracking for example was in itself a complicated business. It soon became clear that there was a distinct and regular form to this pattern, but how to record it? In the laboratory it would be fairly simple for one could bring an egg at certain regular intervals to the photographic apparatus that one had set up specially for the purpose and record the pattern changes as they developed. I didn't have the facilities to do this and so had to resort to written notes and drawings. As it turned out, this method was quite satisfactory, but it was time-consuming and required a certain facility with a pencil.

At the same time I wanted to know what the bird was doing inside the egg which resulted in the pattern of cracking I could see in the shell. So I carefully cut a hole into the air space at the blunt end of the egg so that I could see what was going on inside. The hole was cut with a pointed scalpel very carefully applied to the shell so as to cut a roughly circular groove through the shell without pressing hard enough to crack the shell inwards. The hole itself had to be placed asymmetrically at the blunt end, slightly off-centre, for if I cut directly into the very end of the shell, I thought, I might affect the mechanical strength of the shell in such a way that the hatching process might be interfered with. So I deepened the groove until it broke through at one point and then I was able to insert forceps and break the trapdoor outwards rather than pushing it inwards and risking damaging the duckling.

From the time the embryo was old enough to break through the inner shell membrane I considered that it was advanced enough to be called a duckling. After all, mammalian foetuses can be born very prematurely and grow into normal infants, so by the time an eider embryo is vocalising inside the egg it must be a duckling in all significant factors but environment. So here was the duckling inside the tightly enclosing walls of its shell, ready to escape. But how? When I looked through my observation holes into my eggs (at all other times the holes were covered with tape of course as a protection against dessication or disease) I could see that the bird was crammed in as tightly as an individually packed sardine. In fact more tightly, for it was curled up in such a position that it could move only its head, and that only up and down.

It was already becoming clear to me that successful hatching involves a cracking of the shell around a considerable portion of its circumference. The shell has to be weakened extensively and in a systematic manner before the duckling can push off the end of the egg shell and emerge. How on earth could the duckling make a line of cracks in the shell when it was so tightly enclosed? Well, with patient observation the answer became quite clear, as you will see.

But before I had worked out the hatching mechanism I had discovered to my astonishment that the tapping sounds that come from inside a hatching egg have nothing whatsoever to do with bill-shell contact. They come from inside the bird itself! My observation holes of course enabled me to see what the bird was doing – or at least what its head was doing – and at the same time to hear whatever sound was produced. And it became immediately clear that the tapping, or clicking, is a sound produced by the bird in rhythm with respiratory movements. The click varies in structure, sometimes sharp and metallic, sometimes wheezy, and it varies in occurrence, sometimes on inspiration, sometimes expiration, sometimes both. But it is always, without exception, in rhythm with movement of air through the windpipe. If the respiratory rate increases, so does the clicking rate. If the bird vocalises, the clicking rhythm is the same as the sound rhythm. The immediate causation of the clicking sound is not yet known, but my own feeling is that it is an automatic consequence of the respiratory tubes having air flushed through them for the first time. The mucous materials which fill these tubes while the bird is still an embryo will take some time to disperse, and it sounds like an avian equivalent of a human sufferer from asthma or a bad cold rhythmically breaking a phlegm blockage as he breathes.

If any more evidence was needed that clicking is nothing to do with bill-shell contact, one can hear clicking in newly-hatched chicks or ducklings for several hours, sometimes days, after they emerge from the shell. Dr. W.W.H. Gunn and I recorded this in several species of ducks – and indeed the whole hatching process – at the Delta Waterfowl Research Station in Manitoba before I left Canada. In fact, I have now observed clicking in 24 species of birds belonging to 4 Orders which have precocial young – that is young that can walk or swim soon after hatching. And various people, including myself, have observed it in the young of several species in which the young are relatively helpless and remain in a nest for some time after hatching.

I named this sound "clicking" because that seemed the best

term for it, bearing in mind the quality of the sound. When I returned to so-called civilisation I found that F.S. Breed in 1911 had also used this term for the sound, so I cannot claim priority for the term. But I think I can claim that I was the first to prove conclusively that clicking is directly connected with respiratory movements. In order to establish the connection more clearly than simple observation will allow, I have subsequently, with the help of Dr. R. J. von Baumgarten at the University of Michigan, recorded the clicking sound and the muscular movements of respiration simultaneously. This work was done with the domestic chick. I held a newly-hatched chick comfortably in my hand with a very fine electrode inserted in the pectoral muscles which are involved in respiratory movements. The chick showed no discomfort or distress. The resulting double trace of clicking sound and respiratory muscle movement shows conclusively the direct temporal connection between the two.

So far so good. But the remarkable thing about clicking is that although it seems to be an artefact – an "accident" of nature – it does seem to have an effect upon the synchronisation of hatching of eggs in clutch. Some very interesting work carried out at Cambridge shows, for example, that in eggs incubated separately those which are given a clicking-type stimulus hatch before the others. It was also found that an egg added to a clutch 24 hours late at the beginning of incubation would hatch no more than 6 hours after the others. It seems very likely that the clicking sounds which emerge from eggs after the young bird's bill has pushed through into the air space will serve to accelerate the general activities of any slower-developing eggs in the clutch so that they catch up with the others. It is of course important that young birds such as ducklings should all hatch within a short space of time because the mother duck has to take the brood to water to start feeding as soon as possible after the bulk of them have hatched. If she waited for late arrivals the older ones might be getting weak through having used up the remnants of the yolk store. They can live on this for a day or so after hatching, but have to develop their feeding behaviour as soon as possible. This is probably why one sometimes finds deserted ducks' nests with a hatching egg or a newly hatched duckling left to its own devices. The mother cannot afford to risk the lives of the brood for the benefit of a late hatchling.

Now to return to the hatching mechanism. On the tip of the upper part of the duckling's bill is a hard projection known as the egg-tooth. This is the structure through which pressure is applied

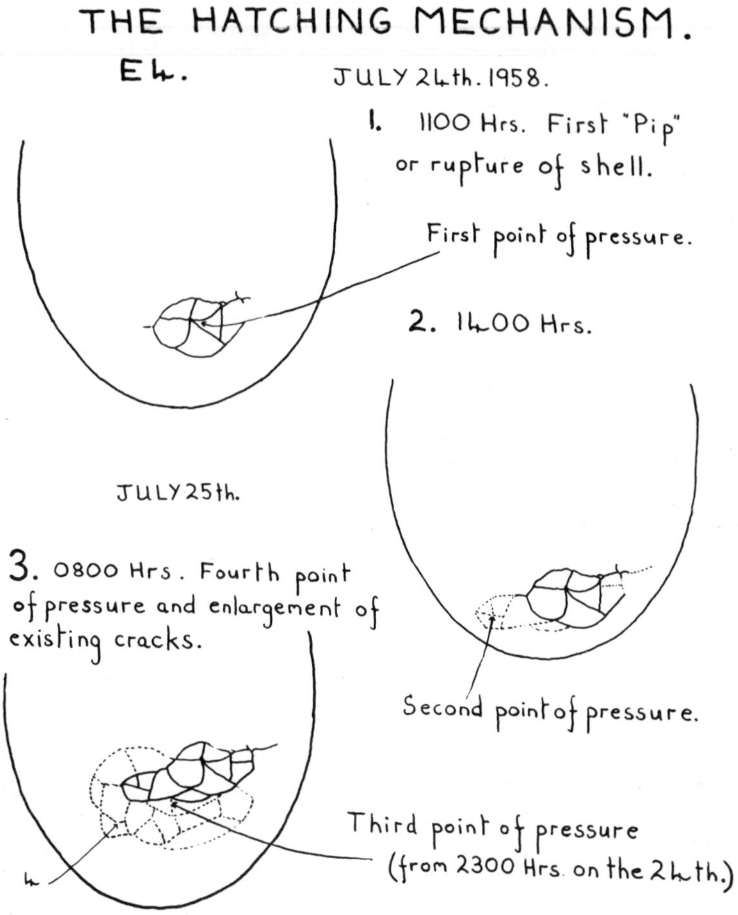

Drawings illustrating the hatching mechanism. By applying pressure to the inside of the shell at successive points with the egg tooth the shell is slowly ruptured.

to the inside of the shell by means of a steady, vigorous upward nod of the head. It also protects the tip of the bill from mechanical damage, for the shell edges at the points of breakage are quite sharp, and in some of my ducklings I noticed that if the bill came into contact with the broken shell edge behind the egg tooth it was likely to be lacerated. When an upward nod is

1

2

Emergence. 1. End view to show amount of cracking. Shell pieces being raised by bill at top centre. 2. Side view to show amount of shell broken off. Membrane is being raised by upward nod at top of crack. 3. End of shell is broken off and bird is beginning to wriggle out.

3

4

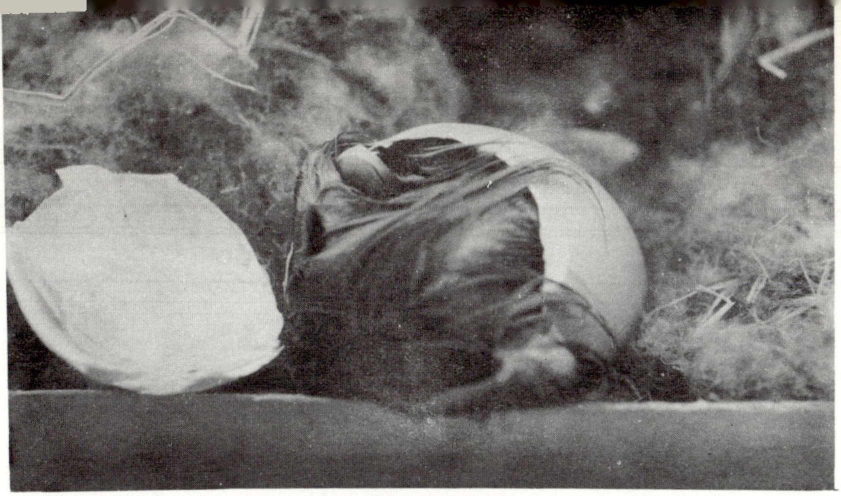

5

4. Perspective view, wings out of shell. Upward nod still being used. Feet not yet free. Calls being given intermittently. 5. Bird free of egg. Note wet and matted plumage, webs still folded. At this stage the bird is still somewhat uncoordinated and highly vulnerable

successful in breaking the shell, the rupture takes the form of a low pyramid of cracked shell with a star-shaped pattern of cracks radiating from the point of pressure. A glance at the hatching drawings will show what I mean. Each pyramid of cracks is known as a pip, and the whole process of shell cracking is called pipping.

So we can see how the duckling – or any other young bird of the precocial sort for that matter, whether they be pheasants, fowl (which are also pheasants really), geese, oystercatchers, or plovers, in all of which, and many more, I have studied this process – how it manages to breach its shelly prison for the first time. But how

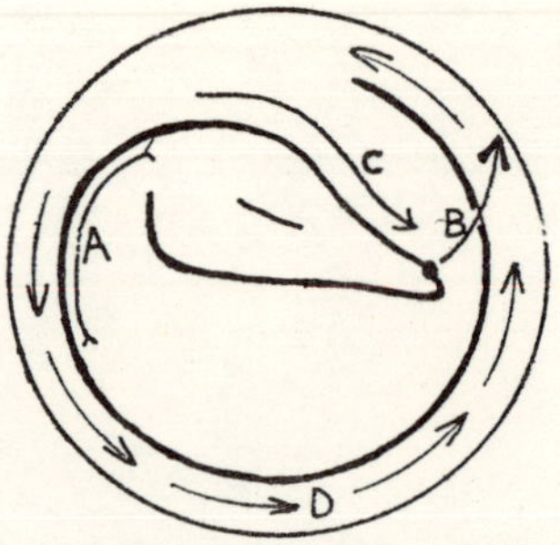

A blunt end view of an egg with young hatching position. Arrows indicate upward nod and turning of body

does it continue the breach around the circumference of the egg until enough of the shell is pipped for it to be able to break off the end? Well, here we have a simply fantastic piece of what T.H. Huxley would have called biological engineering.

As I watched my ducklings through the windows cut in their shells, it soon became clear that subsequent upward nods and therefore subsequent pips tended to proceed in an anticlockwise direction when the egg is viewed from the blunt end. The duckling was turning inside the shell, without any assistance from turning of the whole egg. Indeed, the mother duck sits very tight while her eggs are hatching so she cannot be turning the eggs as she does earlier in incubation.

In order to understand how this can come about we must now consider the detailed and contorted position of the duckling inside the shell. As the first pip is usually in the upper quadrant of the egg, let us assume that the bird's head and bill are horizontal with respect to the ground. The reason that the first pip is near the top of the shell, as it lies in the nest, is probably because the paired muscles at the back of the neck can work most efficiently when the head is horizontal. Anyone who has tried digging sideways with a pick-axe will know what I mean. These paired muscles are specially developed before hatching and are collectively known as the hatching muscle. They run from the back of the skull down the first few neck vertebrae, and by their contraction bring about the vigorous raising of the bill in an upward nod. After hatching the hatching muscle becomes much reduced in size, its principal task being over.

It appears that the duckling, when about to start the hatching process, may not necessarily be lying in the egg with its head horizontal. The head may be on one side, or the other. Or even upside down. Whichever way up it is, however, the duckling starts

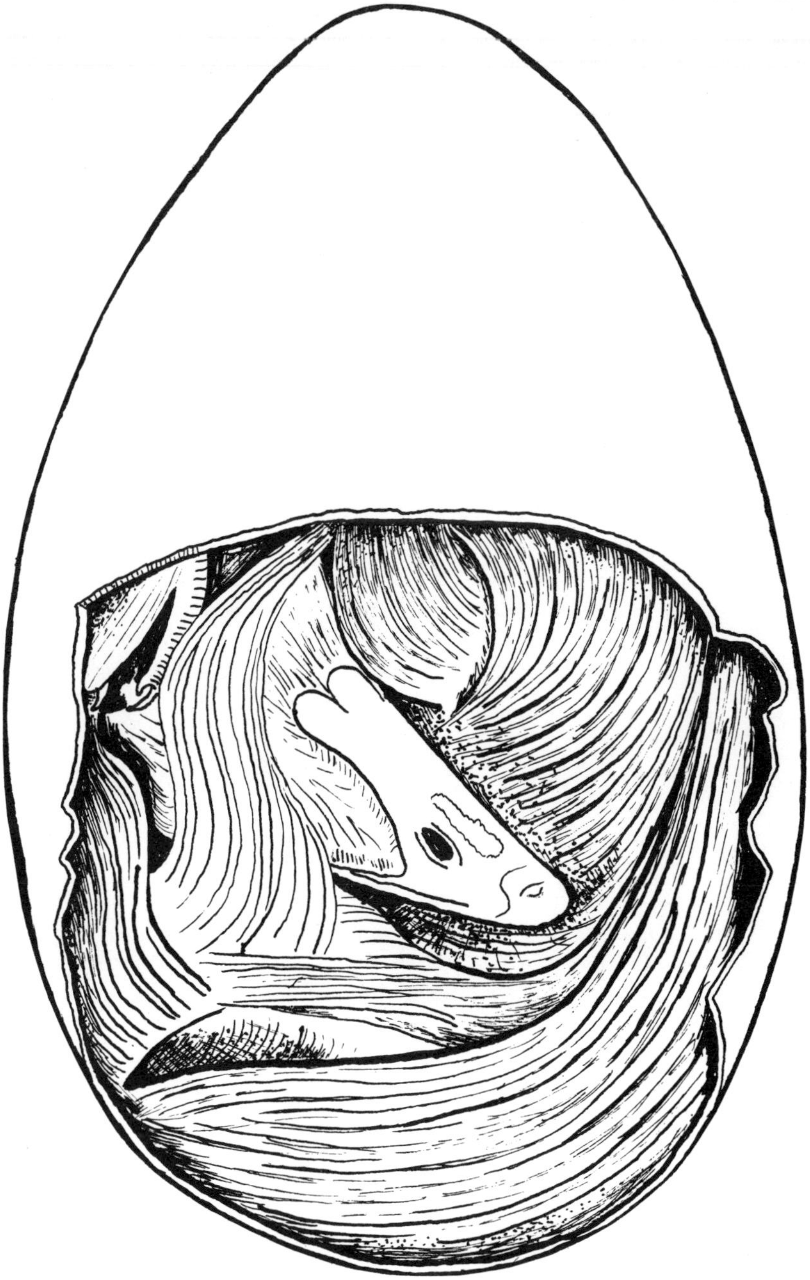

An egg opened to show the position of young about to hatch. The neck is bent and the head lies between the right leg and the right wing

to push its egg tooth against the shell by means of the upward nod. As I will explain shortly, this results in the bird turning around its long axis in the egg, the tail lying in the more pointed end and the body facing the blunt end. When the bird has its head more or less horizontal in the egg it is then in the position where the hatching muscles have the best mechanical advantage for a vigorous push. Hence the first pip is usually towards the top of the egg. In herring gulls Professor Niko Tinbergen found that the next most frequent place for the first pip was on the underside of the egg. In this case, too, the hatching muscles on each side of the neck would be contracting with equal facility. So this may be an exception that proves my rule.

So, having established how the first pip comes to be in the upper part of the shell, we must see how the duckling manages to turn in the shell so that it doesn't push up against the same place a second time. If we can understand the duckling's position in the egg we should be able to see the answer to this problem. Now, although the duckling's tail is towards the sharper end of the egg and its bill is in the blunt end poking into the air space, this does not mean that the bird is stretched out straight from one end of the egg to the other. In fact, when the bird's head is horizontal, so that the upward nod is directly upward with respect to gravity, the bird is lying on its left side. The neck is bent round backwards and then back on itself again so that the head comes to be resting on top of the duckling's right side, in between the right "thigh" and the right wing. The legs are tightly flexed and the bottom joint of the leg points forwards, closely applied to the body, with the right foot lying on top of the head. My drawing of a duckling in the egg will give you an idea of what I mean. In this position the only real freedom of movement which the young bird has is the upward nodding of the head. It can wriggle a little with the wings and it can try to stretch its legs, but these factors are ineffective for pipping purposes.

Because the chick is asymmetrically curled up in the egg in this fashion, when it pushes up against the shell with its bill it puts a torque upon itself and tends to twist around its own long axis. Thus, if one views the egg from the blunt end, each time the upward nod effectively contacts the shell – and not every nod is effective – the bird is inclined to twist in an anticlockwise direction. Thus, the next pip is likely to be slightly "earlier" than the preceding one if we imagine the end of the egg to be a clock face. In this way, in successful pipping, the line of pips proceeds progressively around the blunt end of the egg some distance from the end itself. In eggs with strong shells, such as the ducks and pheasants, around half of the circumference of the shell has to be pipped in this way before the shell is weak enough for the struggles of the chick to break the rest of the shell and open the end as if it were on a hinge. The duckling is then able to uncurl its neck – the urge to do which is undoubtedly one of the factors in the bird's attempt to push up with the bill – and, after a certain interval for rest, the length of which depends on the amount of energy expended in pipping, among other things, the bird scrambles forward out of the shell, leaving behind the excretory sac with its load of uric acid.

The upward nod is an extremely important factor in this hatching process, for it is the only means the bird has of escaping from the shell. It is a very strong movement, and if one removes the shell from above the tip of the bill one can feel the considerable amount of force put into the movement. However, if such a hole is made, the bird is unable to hatch, for the upward nod is the means whereby the bird is enabled to turn in the egg and thereby make a progressive series of pips girdling the egg. Only the very strongest birds can push off the end of the shell with only a quarter of less of the shell broken through. Most of them need half or more. In a few cases the whole of the circumference of the shell is pipped before the bird is able to push open the end.

In some very carefully controlled laboratory experiments I carried out in the University of Michigan to explore this hatching mechanism further, using domestic fowl eggs because they are so easy to acquire, I found that the direction in which the eggs were turned was unimportant, as long as they were turned frequently, and that seven twelfths of the circumference, on average, was the amount that needed to be pipped before emergence. But the pipping sequence always proceeds in an anti-clockwise direction when the egg is viewed from the blunt end. Except in a very small proportion of eggs. And in these cases the chick was the wrong way round in the egg – facing the other end – so these exceptions prove the rule.

Soon after hatching the hatching muscle in the nape of the neck becomes reduced considerably in size. But it does not degenerate altogether because it is used for three other important functions as we shall see in the next chapter. The egg tooth disappears after about two days: pipping is its only purpose in life.

During the relatively short period of time that the duckling has its bill projecting into the air space in the egg before emergence it is able to vocalise. Naturally enough, many of the sounds

Recently hatched and dried out European eider duckling under female's wing

produced under these conditions are what I have called "non-descript" sounds, having no recognisable structure compared with the vocalisations the duckling uses after hatching. But some of the sounds were indistinguishable from those produced by free-living ducklings, and occasionally a duckling still inside the egg could be heard giving the same signal as some of its recently-hatched fellows in the same box. The recognisable signals coming from pre-hatching ducklings included the cohesion call, the complaint, and the distress call. I will describe all six eider duckling acoustic signals in the next chapter. For the moment suffice it to say that these three signals, respectively, serve to assist cohesion of the brood, indicate discomfort, and announce danger or distress. These three signals are those which the female eider pays most attention to and which result in her maintaining or renewing contact with her ducklings. Clearly, if a brooding eider hears these sounds from the eggs beneath her, her attraction to the clutch will be reinforced, with obviously beneficial results. Also, it is known that several species of ducks emit low intensity calls when brooding hatching eggs, and this probably releases vocal responses from the hatching ducklings so that one could say that a primitive type of conversation goes on between the mother duck and her hatching brood. The ducklings in the eggs that I hatched would certainly reply to vocal signals, and also to movements of the egg or tapping on the shell. All of these things are likely to reinforce the female eider's interest in staying on the nest at the critical time of hatching.

The period of hatching of the brood, which may span several hours, is easily the most dangerous time of the ducklings' lives for they are then most vulnerable to predation and exposure. They are relatively helpless as they emerge from the eggs, their coordination of movements taking a little while to develop, and the down being wet and matted making them very vulnerable to cold if the mother does not remain brooding them until they are dry. Presumably this is why a brooding eider, or any other duck, is more loth to leave the nest the nearer her eggs are to hatching. If the eggs are actually pipping, or some young have already emerged, she will stay on the nest until the very last moment, and may perform an injury-feigning display which tends to lure the predator away from the eggs in pursuit of the apparently injured adult bird.

The mother duck's concern for her hatchlings, however, is not the only factor which helps to maintain contact between parent and young. When the ducklings hatch they have become specialists, as it were, in one particular movement – the upward nod by means of which they pip the egg shell. Immediately upon hatching, indeed, while they are actually in the process of hatching, the upward nod takes on another role. It serves to tell the duckling when it is safe beneath the mother. For the duckling has a very powerful urge to push the head upwards into a suitably enclosing structure. As I watched my ducklings hatch, and tentatively explored their reactions to my calls, movements, or touch, I found that by far the most powerful stimulus to the newly-hatched bird was a contact stimulus around the head. The duckling's response – which I call the "brooding reflex" is to stay quite still and quiet, as long as its head is suitably enclosed. Obviously this is a highly functional piece of behaviour. A newly hatched duckling must immediately find the position of optimum warmth and mechanical protection so that it can dry out and stretch itself, and develop the necessary motor co-ordination to enable it to follow the parent when she leaves the nest. The best place for this is nestled in the plumage of the parent, or tucked under her wings or legs. The best way of finding this position – assuming you are hatched under a duck, which is the case with most ducklings – is to push up with the head in an upward nod movement until you feel firm contact around the head. It is all so beautifully simple. The brooding reflex which keeps the duckling in the best place under the female operates automatically as a continuation of the upward nod movement of hatching.

We will explore the brooding reflex and other aspects of the upward nod in the next chapter. As we move from this chapter to the next, the duckling is moving on also. It has escaped from its restricting shell, and is ready to explore the four dimensions of its new environment. This environment is to all ducklings both friend and enemy. Less than half of the ducklings which emerge to nestle beneath the mother eiders will live to pass on the tale to ducklings hatching beneath them. Those that do survive owe much to the brooding reflex. For with that reaction not only do they find a position of security beneath the parent, they also begin the process of imprinting whereby they fixate psychologically upon the parent. The object which satisfies their need for head enclosure becomes the most important object in their little lives. If it moves away they try to follow it and recapture that feeling of security. Without this security they would soon become food for gulls, hawks, owls, or foxes. As in all animals but man, only the fittest survive.

6 The Developing Duckling

During the first few hours or days of their lives certain animals, particularly those which are active from birth or hatching, become psychologically fixated upon the parent in the process known as imprinting. This is particularly well-known in chicks, ducklings, and goslings, but is also seen in other birds and some mammals such as sheep, goats, and cattle. It may even be involved in the formation of the mother-child bond in humans, depending upon how widely one interprets the term.

In nidifugous birds (those that flee the nest soon after hatching), the process of imprinting is particularly important because they do not come into the world already equipped with the means of recognising the appropriate parent animal. As soon as the chicks are dry after hatching, and when the weather conditions permit, the parent takes the chicks from the nest to suitable areas for feeding. If the chicks were not already developing a strong attachment to the parent they would be likely to lose contact both with the parent and the rest of the brood, and the parent would be unable to protect properly a dispersed group of young. Imprinting may be described therefore as a means of promoting the survival of nidifugous, or precocial young, by ensuring that they become psychologically attached to the appropriate parent-object.

As hatching ducklings and other similar birds do not have an inborn ability to recognise their natural parent they may become fixated upon any other relatively appropriate object in their vicinity, and in this way young nidifugous birds have frequently become imprinted to man. Under experimental conditions they may even become imprinted to inappropriate objects, from ping-pong balls to watering cans and nesting boxes. Similarly, when deprived of their natural parents the young of such mammals as sheep, moose, buffalo, and zebra may become fixated upon humans, horses, or motor vehicles.

This tendency to fixate upon the first object which presents itself as a releaser for their filial affections has made ducklings and goslings favourite experimental animals with ethologists. The general process has been recognised as a definite behavioural phenomenon by naturalists from the time of Aristotle, at least, but it was Konrad Lorenz in 1937 who first used the term "imprinting" as a translation of the German word "Pragung". And of course he brought the phenomenon of imprinting to the notice of a great many people in his delightful book *King Solomon's Ring,* first published in English in 1952. It was largely Lorenz's work which enabled me to imprint my ducklings successfully, and I also owe a great debt to the encouragement of Nikò Tinbergen whose Animal Behaviour Research Group at Oxford has made such an important contribution to the development of the science of ethology.

Ducklings are the animals in which the imprinting phenomenon is most clear-cut and in which it is best understood. It has been known for some time that several factors are involved in the establishment of the imprinting response. These include visual and auditory stimuli provided by the parent and also the need to follow the parent when she leaves the nest. Thus a duckling becomes more firmly imprinted the more it has to follow the sights and sounds provided by its mother.

But I found that in my eiders there was an equally – if not more – powerful stimulus which attracted the hatchlings to the parent-object, and this was the tactile stimulus involved in what I have called the brooding reflex. This was so powerful that if I held a hatching duckling's head between my fingers for only a second it would scramble forward out of the egg to push its head in between my fingers again. The method of handling that works best in this respect is with the bird held in the palm of the hand with its bill thrust between the bases of first and second finger and with the thumb providing gentle contact at the back of the head. This method has been effective in releasing the quiescent brooding response in all young precocial birds I have handled whether wild, tame, or imprinted. And my experience of this has covered many species of ducks and geese as well as gulls, plovers, sandpipers, oystercatchers, domestic chicks, pheasant poults, and others. Without exception, this gentle enclosure of the head results in the young bird becoming quiescent, sometimes even closing the eyes and, apparently, going to sleep. In some simple experiments I have carried out with oystercatcher chicks, naturally hatched and,

Newly hatched wild eider duckling showing 'brooding reflex' response of quiescence to gentle contact around the head. Note the egg-tooth at tip of bill

presumably, naturally imprinted, provision of the brooding reflex stimulus around the head resulted in a definite slowing down of the heart beat rate. Oystercatchers are the black and white wading birds common on our coastlines, with striking red-orange bill and legs. The young are precocial but to begin with do not follow the parent, waiting instead for food to be brought to them. Their defence mechanism is to crouch quite still, their ashy-coloured down matching the average seashore background extremely well. If I held one of these chicks in my hand I could feel the heart beating furiously. If I then enclosed the head and bill in my hand, even without covering the eyes, the heart rate would drop considerably.

It seems then that the strong internal drive to push the head up into the enclosing safety of the parent's plumage and the resulting brooding reflex response of quiescence is a very significant factor in the early lives of your precocial birds. Obviously it is of high survival value and instinctive in its nature – that is, the means of behaving in this way is inborn, or innate, and the behaviour is typical of all members of the species.

The brooding reflex may be the explanation of the recent finding that the longer that mallard ducklings stay in the nest after hatching the better they seem to be imprinted upon the parent. It was found that a brood which was forced to stay on the nest for some time because of bad weather conditions followed the parent more eagerly when she left the nest than a brood which, say, hatched early in the morning of a sunny day and left the nest soon after drying out. It could well be that broods staying longer under the female after hatching have become more fixated upon the object that provides them with a brooding reflex stimulus.

Ducklings are hatched, then, with a powerful inborn tendency to become firmly attached psychologically upon the parent-object that provides them with certain tactile, visual, and auditory stimuli. Then, when they leave the nest, the need to follow the parent strengthens that attachment. The nearer the parent object is to the natural parent in its operational characteristics the better the duckling will imprint. Thus a duckling given the choice between, say, the natural parent and a watering can, will choose the natural parent. But the imprinting process does not drive the duckling to fixate upon an individual parent, only upon the parent-object that has the characteristics of the species. This is probably because of the danger of inbreeding which would ensue later, when the duckling reached breeding maturity.

But, as we have seen, if the natural parent is not available the duckling will imprint upon the next most appropriate object. And, during infancy at least, this imprinted preference remains fixed. My ducklings preferred me to female eiders. With this knowledge, based partly upon previous information and partly upon my own work with my ducklings, I was able to imprint my ducklings to myself in such a way that, as far as I was able to tell, their behaviour was as normal as if I had been a female eider. I thus had a wonderful opportunity to observe the development of their normal, natural behaviour.

Birds are largely "instinct" animals, but also have a considerable capacity for learning. My primary task in studying my ducklings therefore – apart from keeping them alive and healthy – was to try to establish the relative roles of instinct and learning in the normal development of their behaviour. This is not easy, for learning processes could be operating immediately upon hatching; indeed, there is a school of thought which claims that the bird is learning certain things while still in the egg. However, the instinct versus learning argument is rather confused and confusing. The important thing is to observe carefully what an animal does naturally and then try to decide whether the terms "instinct" and "learning" are useful in describing normal behaviour, and if so, how and why.

Let me now describe my first observations and experiments to show how I set about my task. These involved my first eider duckling, E.1., hatched on Bladder Island at 2100 hrs. on July 7th. My first observations began at 1200 hrs. the next day and my notes read as follows: "Bird was kept covered until beginning of experiment. Uncovered bird and placed in galvanised bath with 1" depth of water and small aquatic insects. It ignored the latter, floated comfortably, defaecated, sat with beak depressed on breast as ducks do on land. Head sank lower until bill into water – vigorous side-to-side shake of bill released immediately. Function of movement seemed to be clearing nostrils of water. During this time I was immobile and apparently non-existent to the bird. It took very little notice of organisms in water but they did attract its attention three times. Distress call used intermittently – a high-pitched "peep-peep-peep". Comfort notes when removed and brooded – a more rapid, almost twittering "twee-twee-twee-twee-twee". My movements when handling the bird were definite and deliberate but smooth and gentle. It gave hardly any avoidance reaction and I believe that myself and my movements were at this time insignificant to the bird."

"Placed bird on pond. It swam quite comfortably into the

centre of the pond and remained there turning on its axis giving the distress call, as if it were waiting for a signal – a "releaser". I gave the "cow-cow-cow-cow" call of the female and with little hesitation the bird swam directly towards me and out onto the land. It swam most efficiently but walked very clumsily. I crawled slowly away on all fours, calling, and it attempted to follow. Still calling I moved towards it and picked it up. It showed no fear of me at all. Distress call changed to "conversational" notes when it reached land 8 feet from me. I returned bird to its box at 1218 hrs. Distress call when in its box could be changed to "comfort" notes if replied to with female call."

These were my first observations before I had sorted out the different vocalisations of the ducklings, but the notes nevertheless show the kinds of behaviour the duckling is able to carry out on its very first exposure to the natural environment. My second experiment, begun a short time later at 1630 hrs. shows how rapidly the duckling's behaviour patterns develop. Extracts from my notes read as follows: "Bird placed on pond. Occasional movement of myself on bank or my hand near the bird or female calls would keep the bird apparently contented. It began feeding movements first on land, pecking at mosquitoes. Also, the usual duckling nibbling behaviour has been taking place from hatching. The function of this was apparent when 1½ mins after being placed in the water the bird began to nibble at peat on waterline, breaking pieces off and sluicing them in the water. Presumably this could easily result in the ingestion of a food-object. Swimming is presumably released by 'feel' of being in water; nibbling, by proximity of bill to something 'nibbleable'; darting at and seizing in bill, by potential food-object near to head (at least at this stage; later there is a much larger 'catching area'). Movement of object is not essential for release of catching reaction but is definitely a reinforcement, for example, after bird 8 mins in water moving prey appeared to stimulate it to dive in pursuit. Many other times the bird would kick vigorously and almost submerge in its efforts at food capture. Vigorous following definitely released by small animals in water. Food taken included beetles and crustacean larvae. Food seized and rejected included stones, leaves and sticks, after dabbling them in water. Food collecting for first few minutes noticeably more by dabbling than by seizing."

"4½ minutes from beginning of experiment bird efficiently scratched head with foot on land; 12 minutes ditto, efficiently scratched head with foot in water. This was the first occasion for each; thereafter not uncommon."

"Sneezing into water, in the usual anatine way, inserting bill in water and jerking it out again with expiration of air, after 17 minutes. Is the function of this to clear the nostrils? It would tend to do so if there were any obstructions."

"Rudimentary preening movements on first emerging from water. Very good preening on final emergence after 55 minutes, including head rolling and nibbling. Rudimentary bathing movements once after ducking for food."

"Walking on land very good during this experiment. At end of experiment cover blew off box containing bird. Duckling gave distress call, looking around searching the surroundings. When I called, the bird jumped out of its box and into the pond and swam across to me. With the distress call the neck is stretched vertically upwards, with the head as high as possible. This head position is obviously advantageous for searching the surroundings. The bill is opened with each note of the call."

These notes show how rapidly an eider duckling develops efficient survival behaviours on first venturing into its natural environment after hatching. Doubtless other duckling species have similar abilities, as will many other kinds of water birds and also their more terrestrial cousins such as the pheasant family which includes the forebears of our domestic chickens.

Having given an idea of how I collected my information on the development of my ducklings' behaviour, I must now summarise the main aspects of that behaviour, for my notes would fill the whole book. I can only do this, of course, by dealing with the various behaviours in turn, but it must be remembered that the duckling is performing most of these behaviours, as and when necessary, from its first explorations of the environment. Indeed, if this were not the case the bird would not survive, for its feeding mechanisms, vocal signals, and preening movements, as well as its imprinting responses and several other mechanisms, must come into operation within, at the most, the first two days after hatching. Ducklings do not have the security of a nest, as do the perching birds, in which they can remain hidden and relatively inactive, fed regularly, having their excreta removed, and otherwise being tended like infants in a human nursery. The alternative term "precocial" for nidifugous hatchlings is a very apt one. They are the Mozarts, the Bernsteins, the Huxleys of the bird world.

In making suitable responses to its environment, to food objects, to other members of its species, and to its enemies, the newly-hatched duckling is helped considerably by the presence of the female. For example, she will lead the brood to suitable

Ducklings only two hours out of nest showing locomotor coordination and interest in 'potential food objects'

feeding places, brood them when they are cold, and lure or drive away predators. But under equable weather conditions and in the absence of predators she is not essential. This was shown by the survival of the brood of "strangers" mentioned in chapter 4. While they remained near our camp their number remained the same, largely, I believe, because we naturally did our best to keep predators out of our working territory.

Like the other members of its family the eider is hatched at an advanced stage of development that enables it to be self-sufficient from the earliest possible moment. The legs and head are particularly well-developed, allowing for efficient movement and feeding and reception of stimuli through the eyes and ears. The brain is even more highly developed in order to provide for efficient co-ordination and control of behaviour. In fact, from

Imprinted eider ducklings one and two days old showing preening, and interest in 'potential food object' (dark mark on rock)

hatching to maturity, the brain increases in weight about 3 times while the body weight increases around 20 times. As T.H.Huxley noted with respect to a much more lowly animal – the crayfish – the eider when it hatches "possesses in its neuro-muscular apparatus certain innate potentialities of action, and will exhibit the corresponding acts under the influence of appropriate stimuli. A large proportion of these stimuli come from without through the organs of the senses."

The first major locomotor movements the duckling must make are those involved in following the mother duck to water, and we have already seen how the duckling is stimulated to do this. The first walking movements are rather tottery and it is a little while before the duckling can walk well, but they are quite sufficient to carry the bird to water, where it is safer than on land. Once in the water, the duckling is well in control of its movements, being supported by the water and using its webbed feet efficiently. To begin with, as is the case with most of the duckling's behavioural movements, swimming at the water surface is not such a strikingly efficient activity as it is some short time later. For example, the webbed feet are not properly folded on the forward stroke and the amplitude of the stroke is small. But after a couple of hours, or even less, the duckling's surface swimming movements are fully developed, and it can chase mosquitoes across the surface or rush after its mother if she calls, or has moved too far away for the duckling's feeling of safety.

Newly hatched duckling investigating 'potential food object'

From the eider duckling's first hour out of the shell, even while it is drying out and fluffing up its downy coat, it shows a tendency to investigate objects in its vicinity, particularly if they are relatively small, and dark in colour. Thus a newly-hatched duckling may peck at leaves and twigs, another duckling's eyes, anybody's feet, including its own, any beetles, mosquitoes, or other invertebrates which venture near – in fact it pecks at just about anything in its immediate environment that *might* be edible. To begin with a duckling will even peck at its own droppings, with an immediate vigorous shake of the bill and seldom a repeat performance. In the case of my own ducklings the objects they pecked at included ink writing in my notebook, zip fasteners and buttons, the edges of books and boxes, my hair, ears, and bootlaces, and the speckles on herring gull chicks.

The things that release this pecking reaction I have called "potential food objects" because that is just what they are. By experience the duckling learns that some of these objects are edible and others are not. In a very short time the duckling's behaviour changes – if I may put it this way – from processing anything peckable to a process that is quite impeccable. It quickly learns that sticks and stones are not nice to eat but mosquitoes, beetles and water fleas are.

The innate reaction to potential food objects and the rapid learning of their relative edibility result in the ducklings becoming efficient at catching moving prey, such as flying mosquitoes, within the first hour or so of experience. But ducklings cannot live on flies alone, even though I supplemented their diet by slapping my hand to some part of my anatomy every so often and allowed the score or so of mosquitoes and black-flies to fall into the water where they were eagerly snapped up by my charges. For the first couple of weeks of its life, at least, the eider duckling must take a third of its weight in food each day in order to grow properly. Fortunately, it soon learns that there are lots of highly edible food objects swimming around in the water – many more in fact than there are flying above it – including mosquito larvae and pupae, the same young stages of other aquatic insects, and also myriads of various kinds of crustaceans. These last form the bulk of the daily food intake of the very young eiders, my ducklings taking thousands of what we would call "water fleas" and "fresh water shrimps" in colloquial English, very like our *Daphnia* and *Gammarus* respectively. Species of *Gammarus,* moreover, are common on the shore of the sea also, and so whether the mother takes the ducklings first to a tundra pond or the sea shore there is plenty for them to eat. Later they graduate to bigger and better things, but more of that later.

For the moment we are still concerned with the beginnings of the eider ducklings' feeding behaviour. So far they have learnt to take food above, upon, and from just beneath the surface. But they cannot yet dive efficiently enough to pursue this rich source of food beneath the surface.

At this point I must introduce what some ethologists call "fixed action patterns". These are behavioural acts or movements which are always performed in the same way by the same individual and moreover are the same in every other normal individual of the species. They are, as it were, the basic units of instincts. Thus the fixed action pattern of food capture was what I sometimes called in my notes "the capture and sloosh", for it involved a chase, a

Duckling slooshing a horse-fly in water before swallowing it

grab, and a dabble in the water before swallowing. The two-day old duckling is a very adept at this, snatching mosquitoes out of the air, or *Daphnia* from the water, and occasionally grabbing much larger things such as horse flies as they zoom by. In fact, my photograph of the capture and sloosh shows a duckling slooshing a horse fly in the water before swallowing it. The fly was about a third of the size of the duckling's head and must have been flying at 10 m.p.h. at least. Another of my favourite shots is a run of cine film showing a duckling on Nic's head, or actually on his Eskimo tuque to be precise, busily snapping up the mosquitoes crawling and flying on all sides.

Another fixed action pattern, used from the very first time the duckling enters the water, is what I have named "the underwater search". It is the innate method whereby the duckling detects prey beneath the surface, and is seen in very similar form in other species of aquatic birds which hunt in a similar environment for similar prey. In the underwater search posture the neck is stretched forward horizontally at the surface of the water with the eye submerged and the bill beneath the surface at an angle of approximately 30 degrees. This means of course that the duckling can see clearly whatever there is to see down there. If it looked through the surface from just above that surface it would be able to see very little, for the slightest ripple would distort the view. And the water surface is seldom, if ever, without a ripple.

The eyes of birds that capture food underwater have structural

Underwater search posture in eider duckling

modifications to enable them to see clearly in the liquid medium as well as in air. But what I found much more surprising was the fact that the ear is involved in the underwater search posture also. The bird's ear is in rather an unexpected position, to a human, being below and behind the eye. Normally it is covered with feathers of course, but the ear opening is large, and most birds can hear very well.

Eider ducklings spend a considerable amount of time at the surface of the water in the underwater search posture. If the ear opening was submerged, therefore, they might be likely to miss

Underwater search posture in red-breasted merganser duckling

danger signals from the mother or other members of the brood. Which of course would be a distinct disadvantage to the duckling. But the very exactness of the underwater search posture of the head results in the ear opening being tilted up above the surface of the water while the eye is submerged. The duckling can therefore search for its prey beneath the surface, but is still able to receive audible warning of danger. Usually in this posture the webbed feet are spread somewhat sideways and moved together, rather than alternately as in normal swimming, giving extra stability for the head position. Such a simple mechanism, but how important! For a duckling may spend an hour or more a day with its head submerged, which, if it could not hear danger signals, would be of considerable advantage to the gulls and other predators always ready to snatch up any tender unsuspecting duckling.

Remember that I still have the problem of explaining the development of several behaviour patterns which are all appearing and maturing together. Thus we have not yet seen the other functions of the upward nod movement or given a complete account of the duckling's vocal language. But I must interrupt my description of the development of the feeding mechanism of the ducklings to describe the extremely important protective fixed action pattern usually known as the crash dive. As the term suggests, by analogy to the emergency submergence of submarines, this is used as a defence against sudden attack – when the duckling is on the water of course. By its means the duckling can submerge in, literally, a split second. Many, if not all aquatic birds use some sort of crash dive when attacked on water, and all of the ducks, geese and swans, whether diving species or not when adult, use this dive when young.

In eider and old-squaw ducklings, in both of which I have observed the behaviour in some detail, the mechanism of the crash dive is the same. On sudden attack or imminent danger the head is very often first raised on the extended neck in the "alert" or "alarm" posture and the bird immediately begins to submerge. The submergence is brought about by an extremely vigorous kick up and back with both feet together, webs fully spread. At the same time the front of the body is thrust downwards and forwards. There is nothing elegant about the procedure; the bird simply disappears from view with the greatest possible speed and quite a lot of splash. In the case of half-grown old-squaw ducklings the time taken for complete submergence, from sitting on the surface to complete disappearance, is between one quarter and one sixth of a second. This was measured by the simple procedure of counting the number of frames on cine film shot at known speed. As far as I could tell by eye and stop watch the submergence of my eiders was no slower.

Clearly, such a rapid submergence is going to defeat all but the very swiftest or luckiest of predators. But as an added protective bonus, when this crash dive is performed by a group of ducklings they separate under water and reappear scattered over an area of water of anything up to an acre. Also, each individual flight path under water is a quite unpredictable zig-zag. Some wild ducklings, if I surprised them at night by sneaking up to them in my kayak, would actually reappear closer to me than they were when they dived. This is what one would expect if the ducklings simply submerged in the quickest possible manner without respect to which way they were facing on submergence, being primarily concerned with getting down out of danger. These zig-zags, and the unpredictable form of the scatter reactions are examples of "protean" behaviour, that is, behaviour which is so unpredictable in its form or occurence, that it is likely to defeat any potential predator. A gull, or bird of prey, attacking a group of ducklings on the water, cannot learn by experience where they are likely to reappear. Only if the water is exceptionally clear can a flying bird follow the path of the prey beneath the surface and attack it repeatedly as it surfaces, eventually tiring it out. This does not happen often. There is no doubt as to the efficiency of the crash dive as a means of avoiding predators. This has been commented on by many competent field observers and I have observed it myself when one of my own broods was attacked by a gull, and several times when I induced the behaviour experimentally, either by startling my own ducklings or by firing into the water near wild broods.

The mechanism of the crash dive and the scattering after submergence have been the same in all sea-ducklings, and adults, in which I have observed it.

The crash dive is quite innate. All of my eiders and any other newly-hatched sea-ducklings I have observed have used this mechanism efficiently from the first hour or so in the water. Sometimes such a dive is released by a duckling's very first entry into the water, or by a companion diving nearby.

But to return to the feeding mechanisms. We have seen that by means of the underwater search the duckling learns that there are all sorts of food animals swimming around below the surface, many of them out of reach. So it tries to get down to them by kicking itself down through the water. But these attempts are

Early attempts to submerge for feeding

largely unsuccessful. The only way a newly-hatched eider can submerge successfully is by means of the crash dive. But, remember, the crash dive is an innate response to attack, and only to attack. The animal's nervous system is constructed in such a way that the crash dive can only be released by the appropriate stimulus. And in any case, the crash dive involves such a large expenditure of energy that the duckling could not possibly obtain enough food while beneath the surface to supply enough energy for repeated crash dives. If a duckling is forced to crash dive repeatedly it soon becomes exhausted.

So what happens is that over the first day or two's experience in the water the duckling learns to co-ordinate its movements into a highly efficient streamlined feeding dive, a fixed action pattern that takes a little while to mature. Instead of trying to push itself down through the water it gradually changes its tactics to jumping up out of the water first and then taking a smooth header forwards and down. The fully-developed juvenile feeding dive, as I call it, is signalled by a split second intention movement of raising the head in the alert posture, and the bird then kicks vigorously down and backwards with both feet together, webs widely spread, so that it is propelled upwards and forwards. The force of this kick

1

Sequence of movements of juvenile feeding dive, 1 and 2 (3 and 4 overleaf).

2

3

4

is such that the duckling will often jump completely out of the water before taking its header. One can see this quite clearly in some of my cine-film – the bird is completely clear of the surface. David's drawings show the sequence of movements in this dive admirably.

As the duckling re-enters the water it propels itself on downwards with a second bipedal kick, and once beneath the surface its movements are highly accomplished, almost from its first dive. It twists and turns with great agility and develops a remarkably high speed – much faster than when swimming on the surface, though, regretfully, I did not time either. At any rate, the speed of swimming is quite enough to enable the ducklings to catch many prey animals during one submergence, and if one is in the water with the ducklings, as I frequently was, one can see them darting from side to side to take individual swimming crustaceans or insects.

In the case of old-squaw and red-breasted merganser ducklings this underwater swimming ability is even more remarkable, the latter pursuing and catching small fish when only a short time out of the nest. I had two red-breasted merganser ducklings imprinted to myself for a short while, and r.b.m. 2 when five days old pursued, caught, and swallowed 42 small sticklebacks in 15 minutes under natural feeding conditions.

The propulsive mechanism when under water is exactly the same in these three species of diving ducklings – eider, old-squaw, and red-breasted merganser – the webs being spread and used together in a bipedal kick for forward movement, with differential movements of the legs for turning purposes. The wing stubs are not used at all, being held relaxed at the sides. Only in the fully-grown eider are the wings used for accessory propulsion.

The stroke of the legs is in a horizontal plane, the legs, that is, sticking out sideways from the body, and the skeletal structure can be seen to be well-adapted for this, as in other diving birds such as the loons (Gaviidae) and the grebes (Podicipedidae). This makes for much greater manouevrability than would be the case if the legs moved in the vertical plane as in walking birds. It is also, of course, one of the reasons why water birds are so clumsy, relatively speaking, on land.

The juvenile feeding dive is clearly the best way for the duckling to submerge if it is not in a desperate hurry. The two separate bipedal kicks – the one as it jumps up from the water and the other as it re-enters – are approximately half a second apart, the time taken for submergence by means of this dive being between half and threequarters of a second. The reason for the development of this dive would seem to be the very young duckling's high buoyancy. When they stop swimming beneath the surface they come shooting up like corks. To push this buoyant object down through the water is just too much for them except in an emergency, and the extra impetus derived from the jump out of the water is just what is needed. Later, as the duckling grows and becomes rather like a farmyard duck in bulk and shape, it is so heavy, particularly at the front end of the body, that it simply has to put its head and neck down into the water and push itself on down. But that comes much later. The very young duckling is obliged to develop the juvenile feeding dive in order to submerge, and indeed, in order to survive. That is why it has become part of the duckling's instinctive repertoire.

Once the juvenile feeding dive has developed properly the duckling begins to put on weight steadily. But its energy requirements during feeding are such that much of the weight it puts on during the day is lost overnight. So the young eider's life consists of an endless succession of feeding sessions, interspersed with periods of preening, drying out, and resting. I weighed my ducklings twice a day, in the morning before feeding, and again in the evening after the day's feeding sessions were over, and it became clear that they needed at least 8 hours a day in the water for feeding purposes if they were to grow properly. In our first season, alas, I did not realise this basic fact – I was not yet experienced enough for proper eider motherhood – and my ducklings lost weight and died after about 10 days. In my second season I knew better and gave my broods enough time in the water for the collection of sufficient food for their needs.

In case anyone is thinking that I was rather callous with my first brood, I can assure them that their deaths affected me emotionally as well as intellectually. I had become genuinely attached to them. But, remember, I was investigating the development of their natural feeding mechanisms and if I had supplemented their diet with artificial food at an early age I would have missed much of importance in the development of their behaviour. In our second season I gave them as much time in the water as was necessary for proper growth until I was sure I had seen the principal factors in the development of their behaviour. Only then did I change them over to artificial food – turkey starter crumbs – which we had taken with us for the purpose. In any case, if I hadn't done that I might have finished up thinking that I really was an eider, not just a substitute. When you have spent two or three weeks behaving

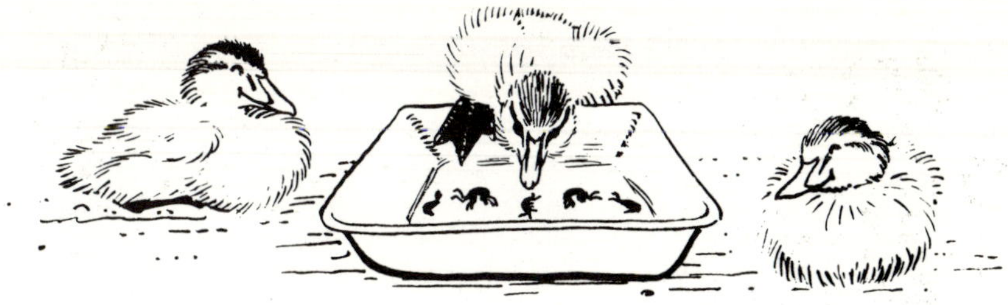

like an eider duck, you have a tendency to think like one and to shun other humans. I must have been rather difficult to live with during those days.

After a couple of weeks in our second season it was becoming clear to me that the feeding behaviour of the ducklings was the principal key to their survival, and I decided to try some opportunistic experiments to investigate this further. I conditioned E.9, E.10, and E.12 – Eddie, Edie, and Ada – to feeding from a large aluminium tray upon which were placed living *Gammarus* (the crescent-shaped water shrimps that scuttle along on their sides) in a film of water deep enough for them to move around normally. The ducklings soon learned to paddle around on the tray slooshing up this apparently endless supply of food in what must have been to them an alimentary paradise. It was quite fun for me too. But poor Nic, who had to keep up with the ducklings' apparently insatiable appetites, turning over stones on the shore to catch thousands of *Gammarus* had rather a rough time of it.

Anyway, once the ducklings were accustomed to feeding in this way I began the experiments proper, concentrating on Edie and Ada, as Eddie was rather poorly and in fact died a few days later for reasons which I was unable to discover. I wanted to find out how many *Gammarus,* and their total weight, a hungry duckling would take at one sitting until gorged. This I did by dropping *Gammarus* one or two at a time onto the tray occupied by a waiting duckling, at a rate adjusted to their maximum speed of disappearance into the duckling. The *Gammarus* were taken from a polythene container, previously weighed, and any gravel that happened to drop with the crustaceans was returned to the container before the final weighing. Also the bird was weighed before and after the session. Edie and Ada each had seven sessions of this situation, over a period of eight days, and showed a remarkable capacity for *Gammarus.* Their rate of intake tended to

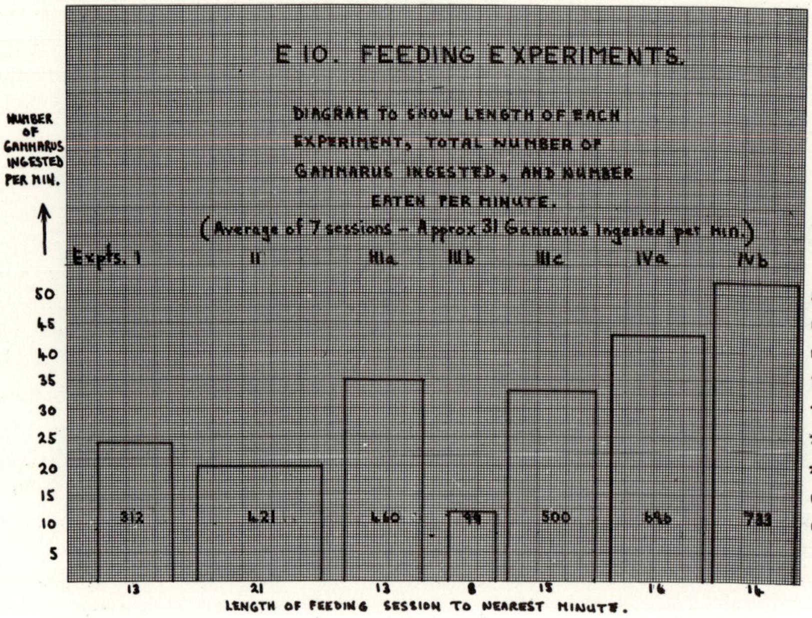

increase from session to session, partly no doubt, through a simple learning process, but also, I think, because they were getting more hungry. My daily weighings showed that they did not do so well with this mass intake at long intervals as with a steady intake of smaller numbers over a longer period of time under natural conditions. However, their intake was truly astonishing, Edie holding the record with 733 *Gammarus* caught and swallowed in 14 minutes during her seventh experimental session. The average, for both birds, of the seven sessions was 31 *Gammarus* taken per minute. In her record session Edie increased her weight from 201 grams to 259 grams, showing, incidentally, what a large amount of food can be stored in the duckling's crop. Under natural feeding conditions this would often be of considerable advantage, for some of the summer tundra pools are thick with swimming crustaceans, and it is obviously to a duckling's advantage to take in as much as possible while the going is good. However, the principle of taking smaller amounts of food at a time more or less continuously is obviously the best, as shown by the ducklings' decrease in weight during the experimental feeding period and the normal behaviour of all ducklings under natural conditions.

After a few weeks of feeding principally upon small crustaceans, eider ducklings gradually change to a diet of molluscs. It is well-known that adult eiders feed largely upon molluscs such as the edible mussel, *Mytilus,* the hard shells being crushed by the very muscular gizzard with the aid of small stones and gravel deliberately swallowed for the purpose – though we cannot assume that this means that the bird realises that this is why it has such an interest in swallowing gravel. At the age of 4 to 5 weeks my ducklings showed a noticeably increasing interest in molluscs, diving or up-ending to search the bottom for objects of small mollusc nature. Observations of other workers on the stomach contents of eider ducklings from 3 or 4 weeks old show a distinct preponderance of *Mytilus* and similar molluscs. The change to a mollusc diet before fledging – the time when the ducklings begin to fly – would seem to be essential.

Now we must return to our consideration of the upward nod movement in the behavioural repertoire of the young eider. We have seen that this is the means whereby the duckling hatches, and

Two day old eider duckling (centre bird) giving greeting

that the same movement is instrumental in the duckling achieving a position of optimum protection beneath the mother. But as soon as the duckling leaves the nest with its fellows and mother the upward nod takes on another extremely important function. In conjunction with a special call, the "cohesion call", the upward nod is used as a greeting, indicating to its fellows and parent that "I am a friend, and one of you". From their first outings my ducklings would use this greeting to each other and to me. Whenever contact was rejoined after a temporary separation, or when I gave the female cohesion call, or the ducklings came hurrying back to me after being scared or left behind, the greetings would be given consistently. The cohesion call is also used separately – a rising twitter of, usually, four notes – apparently serving to maintain the cohesion of the brood; hence its name. We will consider this call again later, together with the other vocalisations.

The remaining function of the upward nod movement is in drinking. Most birds drink by dipping the bill tip into the water and tilting the head up so that the small amount of liquid contained in the bill is tipped down the throat. This movement in eider ducklings is almost indistinguishable from the upward nod of the greeting, but of course it is not confused with the greeting because in the latter the movement is accompanied by the cohesion call. In the uses of the upward nod, therefore, we have a fine example of biological economy. The four different upward nod functions are separated contextually so that there can be no confusion between them in the signal sense. With, presumably, relatively little increase in brain complexity, the same muscular movement can be used for four quite distinct items of behaviour which are essential for survival.

And now we must consider the vocalisations which have been mentioned from time to time. There are six of these, all innate – that is, they are used automatically, without learning, as soon as they are needed. And because they are common to all eider ducklings, and similar in all, we can assume them to be, by definition, "instinctive".

The distress call mentioned earlier is very similar to the distress call of other ducklings. In eiders it is a repeated monosyllable, high-pitched and piercing, with great carrying power, and may be repeated indefinitely until the distressing situation is relieved. This call is used when the duckling is in serious difficulties; for example when it is very cold, being attacked, is very hungry, is lost, or left far behind. The reaction of the mother is to come to the aid of the duckling if at all possible. This call and the cohesion call are the only two eider duckling vocalisations clearly described before my own work revealed the others.

A call which, apparently, had previously been confused with the distress call is that which I call the 'complaint''. This is a disyllabic call with the second note rising, insistent and tending to be indefinitely repeated, but not so piercing as the distress call. The complaint is given by a duckling which is in difficulties but not in such serious situations as those which give rise to the distress call. For example, it is heard when the duckling is cold but not desperately so, when it is hungry but not starving, when it is left behind but not in danger of getting lost, or when an attack seems likely but not imminent. This makes excellent sense from the evolutionary point of view, for if the mother were to come rushing to the aid of a duckling in all circumstances of discomfort she would soon become worn out and unable to perform her duties properly when the ducklings were in real danger. The effect upon the parent is to alert her to the situation so that she is aware that all is not right with her brood and can take any necessary action if the situation becomes serious.

The twittering, rising cohesion call has already been mentioned, serving to maintain the cohesion of the brood because it is given by the ducklings whenever they are not specifically motivated to produce any other of the vocal signals. The cohesion call is a good name for it because if a duckling becomes momentarily separated from its fellows – say, behind a rock, or around a corner – this is the call it is most likely to hear and it therefore proceeds in the direction of the sound and regains contact with the brood.

It seems clear that the cohesion call had previously been confused with what I have named the "contentment call". This is, on first hearing, similar to the cohesion call, being a phrase of four rapidly repeated notes, but the phrase tends to be faster, higher pitched, and less rising in pitch than the cohesion call. It is produced by the duckling when the bird has just taken in food, or is comfortably preening with its fellows. Thus a sequence of calls from an individual duckling on a pond, diving and feeding with its fellows, might go as follows: cohesion, cohesion (dive and capture food – surface), contentment, contentment, cohesion, cohesion (dive again for food) and so on. With this knowledge of infant eiderese I was able to know what my ducklings were about even when I lay dozing on the bank in the sun. Their vocalisations indicated exactly what was going on, all of them being instinctive and therefore only being released in certain specific circumstances.

Similarly, if I surprised a brood of ducklings at night on the water and they crash dived and scattered while the mother sped away, as the ducklings surfaced I would hear distress calls, then complaints as they located the mother some distance away, then cohesion calls as the brood was eventually re-united.

Perhaps the most unexpected of all the eider duckling vocalisations was that which I have called the "query-alert". At first I called it the "question", but an eminent professor of psychology considered this too anthropomorphic, and suggested I call it the "investigatory note", which, for a while, I did. But for reasons with which I hope you will agree I now call it the query-alert. This is a thin, rising, and to human ears at least rather a faint single call, seldom heard more than once from a particular duckling on any single occasion. In my first season as an eider I heard it only on one occasion and had difficulty in categorising it, as you may judge from my notes of the occasion which were as follows: "I sat on usual rock. Bird fed avidly on mosquitoes on vertical rock surface near to water. It must take 100 plus at each feeding bout. Also taking crustaceans in water. Once, bird got some long grass caught around its neck and dragging behind it as it swam. It gave quite a different call from normal – a questioning, rising, short, monosyllabic 'peeip?'. It swam towards me when I called and stayed quite still while I removed the obstruction." This was with E.2 on its 14th outing when it was five days old.

Next summer I heard this call on several occasions from both my own eiders and wild broods. Sometimes my ducklings would give the call if a human other than myself appeared. At other times they would give it in response to a distant view of a large bird in the sky – a potential predator perhaps. Or wild eiders would give the call if they saw me at some distance away: not near enough to be dangerous but perhaps needing watching. It looked very much as if this was a call which would alert other members of a brood, and possibly the female as well, to something unusual, not obviously dangerous but possibly so. If this is the case it is one of the most interesting instinctive calls I have come across, because it is a reaction to something without clearly recognisable or definite characteristics. Here is a beautiful case for experimental study.

Finally, in the eider duckling's acoustic repertoire, we have the "brooding note". This is the call I am sure many people have heard from ducklings being brooded under the mother duck or, perhaps, a bantam substitute. And in the case of my ducklings they would sometimes give this call when being brooded by me inside my shirt or sleeping bag. The brooding note is a rich and satisfying-sounding call – one can't help being anthropomorphic here – it does really sound like that – of a single rising or falling note. I assume, though this too needs experimentation, that it is a reinforcement to the brooding mother to stay put, meaning "I feel pretty good"!

By means of the various instinctive behaviours described so far, perhaps with the help of learning processes which make them

Two day old duckling, sodden after diving for food. It emerged to sit and preen with its human 'mother'

optimally efficient, the young eider is able to interact with its environment – including its fellows and mother – so that it is able to feed and grow properly. But this means diving and feeding under water for many hours a day, and this, in turn, means that the ducklings get wet. So they must preen in order to dry out, clean up, and rearrange the plumage.

In adult birds preening movements are based upon the necessity to restore the physical continuity of the vane or web of each feather. As you probably know, a feather is made up of thousands of filaments all joined together by little hooklets so that the complete and tidy feather makes a continuous surface, and the sum of these continuous surfaces makes a complete and tidy bird. A preening bird also oils its feathers as it is re-arranging them by rubbing its bill and head on the oil gland at the base of the tail and then rubbing that oil off again on various sections of the body feathers. The head is dealt with by scratching because, of course, a bird cannot reach the top of its head with its bill.

The downy plumage of ducklings is not so complex as the fully-developed feathers of the adult, and probably not as efficient, for ducklings seem to get their plumage soaked through much more quickly than the adults do, and therefore have to preen more often. In fact, most feeding sessions of a few minutes to half an hour or more are followed by preening and drying-out sessions on the bank. A sodden duckling is a very bedraggled object, being unable to keep itself warm in the water or on land, and also being less buoyant in the water. The early development of efficient preening is therefore of crucial importance to the duckling and preening movements can be seen from the very beginning. To start with – that is, for the first few minutes, or dozens of attempts at a particular movement – the preening movements do not do their job very well. The duckling will aim its bill at some part of its anatomy, for example, and not quite make it. But the general procedure improves very rapidly, indeed it has to, and the duckling is soon preening itself dry after every session in the water.

Only if the weather is very warm and windless will a wet duckling not bother to preen very much. Normally a definite set of preening fixed action patterns is completed, the water being squeezed and worried out of the down and the fluffy surface restored. The principal preening movements are oiling, and scratching, which have already been mentioned; nibbling, which re-arranges and removes water from the smaller feathers; stropping, which performs the same function for the large feathers; and

Eider duckling preening

head-shaking, which removes from the bill the water squeezed out of the plumage.

Bathing is also seen from an early stage, but would not seem to be so crucial to the very young bird. It too involves a series of fixed action patterns (the theorists who don't like the term "fixed action pattern" will be getting wilder and wilder!), the principal ones being shuffling, by means of which water is shuffled over the back; ducking, which is the sinuous and head-first immersion of the body; and flapping, which is a simultaneous beating of the wings which seems to assist in the general wettening process.

It might be wondered why ducklings bathe in order to get wet when they have to preen so much in order to get dry! There are probably two main reasons for this. First, during the duckling's underwater explorations and pursuits it is bound to get fouled up to a certain extent with various bits of aquatic plants and general debris floating around in the water. And second, the various bathing movements would seem to loosen the feathers up and get water into all the crevices, as it were, so that the preening movements can then have a fair start. Rather like grooming of the human head. It is best to have one's hair washed before having it set. Or so I am told.

The author with duckling brood. The one nearest is pedalling

And now, finally, before passing on to the chapter concerned with adolescence and adulthood, I want to consider one of the most intriguing of eider duckling behaviour patterns. I call it "pedalling". I have only studied it in detail in four of my own birds, but I have seen wild ducklings doing it, as well as adults, and their observers have seen it in various species of sea-ducks. I call this behaviour pedalling because that is just what it looks like – as if the duckling is sitting on an imaginary sit-up-and-beg bicycle in the water, pedalling like mad but getting nowhere. One of the curious things about it is that it did not appear in my ducklings until they were 8 days old. The first time I saw this curious movement I thought the bird was going out of its tiny mind. But it continued to do it almost each time it went into the water. And then when the other three ducklings reached the age of 8 days they started to do it too! So it seemed that here was another example of a fixed action pattern, but one that needed 8 days of post-hatching life in which to mature.

During typical pedalling the duckling sits up in the water moving the legs and feet almost in the vertical plane but with incomplete folding of the webs in the up-and-forward stroke so that if there is any forward movement of the duckling at all it is slower than usual. It really does look, at first, as if the bird is

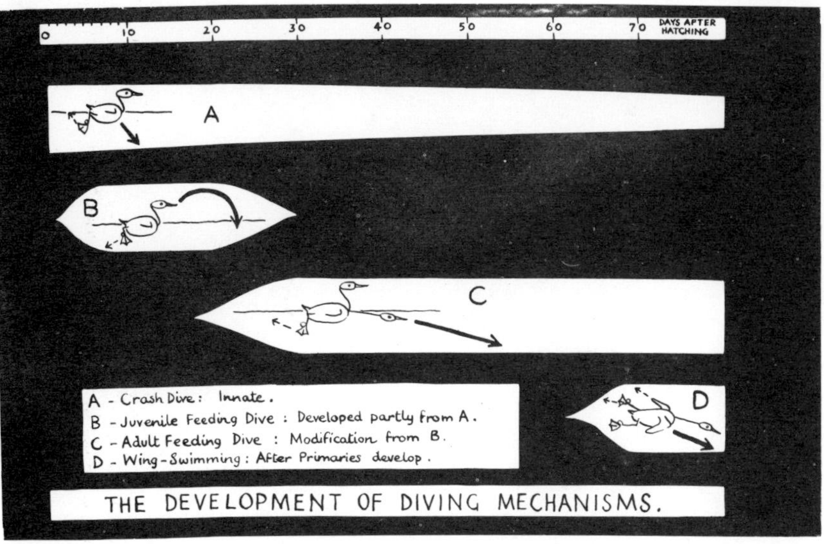

The development of diving mechanisms in eider ducklings. The size and shape of the different panels indicate the relative importance of the various mechanisms at different ages

demented, for it seems to have no function, and when the bird starts to do it, it appears to be a behavioural accident. As I watched my birds pedalling in shallow water, however, I noticed that the movement of the webs would often stir up the bottom. This could reveal food organisms which were otherwise concealed. As pedalling continues, therefore, interspersed with bouts of diving and underwater searching, the duckling is going to benefit from pedalling by capturing more food than it otherwise would. And it may be that the duckling eventually learns to pedal in order to stir up food organisms from the bottom – but that is as yet unproven. That it does assist feeding is almost certain, for I have seen adult females pedalling with ducklings diving around them, and other ethologists have seen this too.

At the age of 3 to 4 weeks the ducklings begin to show considerable independence and from this time one can say that they are, as it were, teenagers. Adolescence seems to begin with the increase in bulk which enables them to dive down through the water without having to take an athletic leap out of the water first. The process is gradual, of course, but the five week old duckling, diving in a few fathoms of water perhaps for mussels, is quite a different animal from the little balls of down cuddled beneath the mother's feathers – or shirt – an hour or so after hatching.

7 Releasing the Apron Strings

"And Merlyn had taught him about animals so that the single species might learn by looking at the problems of the thousands."
T.H. White: The Once and Future King.

A number of behavioural biologists have drawn attention to the dangers of making facile comparisons between the behaviour of man and the other animals. So many factors are involved in any one behaviour pattern in any one species of animal that comparisons with other animals are fraught with difficulties in interpretation. But the fact remains that we, no less than the other animals, have developed the basic fundamentals of our behaviour patterns as the result of the pressures and processes of natural selection operating upon our forebears. It is true that much of human behaviour is the result of environmental influences operating upon the individual in his own lifetime, in the home, the school, and in the wider cultural sphere. Nevertheless, there is no real evidence to support the suggestion that there is no longer an instinctive basis to our activities, while there is plenty of theoretical, observational, and comparative evidence to suggest that our complex learning abilities and intelligence faculties are part of a superstructure built upon instinctive foundations. We at least seem to share with the other mammals and with the birds the basic "instincts" of sleeping, mating, feeding, and grooming, and it is likely that we have much in common also with respect to aggressive, defensive, and social behaviours.

It is certainly true that in all birds and mammals that care for their young there is a period during which the stage of dependence upon the parent is replaced by independence of the young. This period varies in length according to many factors in different species but the general process is similar in all: from the stage of being a juvenile more or less dependent upon the parent, the animal moves through a stage of adolescence to a stage of adulthood and, normally, parenthood, with young of its own to care for.

With human children of my own, and having taught at all high school and university levels, I believe I have a fairly good general picture of the behavioural as well as structural changes involved in human adolescence. Not that such experience naturally gives one such understanding, but I have the good fortune to be a naturalist and trained scientist as well as a teacher with an interest in people, and I therefore observe and register more than most people of what goes on around me. This is not a boast; plenty of other naturalists will understand what I mean. As I have pointed out elsewhere, the average successful peasant farmer knows more about the normal behaviour of the animals with which he comes into contact than the average professor of psychology: not because he is more intelligent but because he has to be observant in his work and he is in close contact with animals for more of the time. When, therefore, the behaviour of my adolescent ducklings reminded me forcibly of that of human adolescents, I was not only fairly confident of the relative objectivity of my observations but also inclined to take seriously the possibility of comparisons.

Clearly, in those animals that begin their lives completely dependent upon their parents and then switch, sooner or later, to almost complete independence, some definite change must be taking place in the animal's internal control systems – neurologically at least. And these changes will be made obvious in the visible changes in behaviour between those animals and their parents. In man, for example, there is a definite parental response to animals with a high "fubsy index" – not only teddy bears, kittens, puppies, toy poodles, and Bambi, but also the young of many other animals, particularly birds and mammals. The "fubsy index" is a term referring to what Konrad Lorenz pointed out as long ago as 1943 as the sum of the specific sign stimuli which release parental responses in man: a short, round-cheeked face in relation to an expansive forehead, and stumbling, poorly-coordinated limb movements. These various factors can be summed to make a fubsy index which reflects the extent to which parental responses in man are released by the species concerned. Of course human children have the highest fubsy index with respect to normal adults, but baby birds, particularly chickens and ducklings, and baby rabbits, lambs and goat kids, in addition to those already mentioned release similar responses. Hence the predilection of childless women for pekes and other animals with high fubsy indices. And when I show my film or slides of my ducklings – although they are not technically very good – there are always parental "ooh!" and "aah!" responses from at least some of the females in the audience. I'm sure you will all know what I mean. But is is interesting that a soft downy, woolly, or furry covering makes the animal even more cuddly, for human babies are effectively naked. Perhaps this is something that goes

A young eider duckling has a high 'fubsy index'

way back into our past when we were still hairy, and babies were covered with a soft downy fur.

Adult animals, including humans, do not release parental responses in other adult humans unless the "releaser" animal happens to have a high fubsy index as the result of natural or artificial selection for some other purpose, as in budgies and pekes respectively. Also, the complexity of human culture cometimes results in women developing accentuated attractiveness to men as a result of the development of certain fubsy index factors, for example the transient fashionable interest in "helpless" or "baby-faced" women. And it is only reasonable that these examples should be exceptions rather than the rule, for the interactions between adults must of necessity be very different from the interactions between adults and their young. Exceptions to this rule are only seen in ritual or malfunctional human contexts. As a species we are nowhere near the state of understanding of behavioural processes that would enable us to replace our natural, evolved behavioural interactions with something that might be thought to be more appropriate in the technological age. And there is considerable evidence to suggest that technological society itself is becoming so disorganised that we should perhaps consider it as a failure rather than as progress. So perhaps we can learn something to our advantage by studying other animals in which the numerous behavioural malfunctions seen in contemporary humans do not operate. I would certainly say that the average adult eider is more contented – in its fashion – than the average human adult is in the human sense.

However, to use a play on words developed by James Fisher, I must return from word botching to bird watching, and describe the signs of adolescence I observed in my eiders. The most anthropomorphic of these signs was the behaviour I described in chapter 4 when my ducklings were quite well-grown and their flight feathers were at last developing. Much wing-flapping goes on at this time, with the duckling almost standing up in the water – "Finding its feet", as it were in human terms, though "finding its wings" would be more appropriate. At this stage they still preferred to stay around the camp area, if allowed to swim off on their own, but were moving further and further away each day before returning to the security of "home". This "home" was not the place itself, but me, to whom they were imprinted. And then came the time when they would not come ashore in the evening and we had to go out onto the water in the boat and shepherd them ashore. But all this time they were performing the ritualised upward nod and twitter of the greeting ceremony. I was strongly reminded of the human teenager who still says "hi!" if meeting adults in the street or wherever but is now quite well able to look after himself and would rather you left him alone.

But adolescence is not something that happens suddenly. It may be *noticed* or brought to one's attention suddenly, but one is then simply perceiving a late stage in a process which has been going on for some time. Just as we begin to die as soon as we are born – our organs and metabolism only having a certain potential of growth and replacement – so do we approach, pass through, and leave behind adolescence as we proceed from infancy to adulthood. After all, what is maturity? It can be argued that many people never reach that stage, having been diverted on the way by some quirk of upbringing or inheritance that denies them anything like the realisation of their potential development. In ducks the situation is much simpler, the adult organism being far less complex than the human and operating within certain definable limits. We do not yet know the potential of the human mind or culture, but in eiders we can state pretty well all the more important factors which influence the animal and describe the animal's normal reaction to them. In no sense can an eider choose what reaction to make to its fellows, its enemies, or its environment. It has evolved along a line which adapts it as nearly perfectly as is possible to its environment, but this does not involve freedom of choice. Its behaviour is pre-programmed in the sense that it is hatched with a brain that in the successful individuals will pilot the animal through its life by instructing it to do certain things automatically without previous experience of the circumstances ("instinctive" behaviour) and to learn by experience to do other things automatically (learning behaviour). It does not have the mixed fortune to possess anything like human "intelligence" (and whatever that is is a matter of considerable controversy). Instinct and learning, or that fascinating combination of the two processes which results in the animal developing appropriate responses to certain environmental features which it has an innate interest in exploring, are quite enough for the successful operation of animals other than humans.

As adolescence is a gradually developing and waning process it would be quite arbitrary to say that the process begins or ends with any particular behaviour or at any particular point in time. This reflects one of the exciting and challenging things about biology – most biological processes cannot be categorised in the same way as physical or chemical ones, as definite measurements, discrete quantities, or invariable qualities. Nevertheless, we can say that before a certain point an eider duckling has not reached adolescence proper, and after another point it has passed adolescence. I would say that an eider duckling actually begins to demonstrate the release of the apron strings when it has become accustomed to sleeping without its head being enclosed in the female's plumage. You may remember that the feeling of head enclosure is very important to a very young duckling, the "brooding reflex" being the mechanism by which the duckling rests quietly once it has gentle contact stimulus around the head. But as the duckling grows – and the healthy ones grow very quickly – it soon becomes too big to nestle beneath the female. But the brooding reflex would seem to be still operative in quite large ducklings, for they will stay quiet – at least for a while – if the head or bill is gently enclosed in the hand.

Now, the first true feathers to develop in eiders are the scapular

Four week old eider with scapular and flank feathers developed

Seven week old eider sleeping with bill under scapulars

feathers — the feathers over the shoulder area which smooth out the depression where the limb emerges from the body. A month-old duckling — which has increased its weight from about 60 grams to around 600 grams — is clearly too big to brood under the female. But by this time the scapulars are well developed and the duckling sleeps with its head tucked under them, or with the bill enclosed at least. So from about 3 weeks of age the duckling is learning to sleep by itself, as it were. The brooding reflex stimulus is now provided by its own feathers instead of those of the parent or the numerous "aunties" which eider ducklings have, broods often being interchanged. A one or two week old duckling sleeping alone has nothing into which it can tuck its head when sleeping, and looks very forlorn dozing with its bill tip resting on the ground. But of course ducklings of this age would not survive on their own under natural conditions. I happen to have noticed this bill-on-the-ground posture because I had isolated ducklings for short intervals. Thus the onset of sleeping with the bill tucked into the scapulars was brought to my attention more forcibly.

By this time — 3 to 4 weeks after hatching — eider ducklings are normally well-adapted to feeding upon molluscs for which they dive off shore, and have already become accustomed to the mode of feeding typical of the adults. They are therefore all set for adulthood, except for the fact that the parent bird or birds provide useful experienced lookouts and guards. But, in common with most birds, the longer the duckling lives the greater its life expectancy, for most mortality is in the first week or two of life. As they get older, therefore, they become more experienced in recognising and dealing with dangers. But then comes the time

One week old duckling dozing

Footprints of young and adult eiders

when they must fly. The flight feathers are the last to develop and the bird is not ready to fly until it is ten weeks old or more. While it is "finding its wings" the adult birds must still be of considerable help to the adolescent bird, if only for their warnings of approaching dangers while the offspring is concentrating on its new-found freedom (human comparisons are very tempting here!).

But when the young bird has learnt to fly, can we then say it is adult? Hardly so in the case of eiders, for it takes 3 or even 4 years for the drakes to develop their full breeding plumage, without which they cannot display properly and mate. So although they are probably physiologically capable of fathering ducklings at 2 or 3 years of age they stay bachelors for a while after adolescence. Some of them may attempt to mate but they don't get very far in competition with males in full finery. We can be fairly sure that they suffer no humanoid frustrations during this period for their bird brains are not "advanced" enough to allow disturbances equivalent to those of the human psyche in a disturbed cultural environment. The eider post-adolesent has an easier time of it than many of its human counterparts.

I want to conclude by seeing if our journey into eiderland can teach us anything about the nature of the living animal and if this understanding can have any relevance to the contemporary unsettled human condition. We have seen that an eider at any age is in a state of transition: from egg to juvenile, from juvenile to adolescent, from adolescent to immature, and from immature to mature adult. Also, the species as a whole is in a transitional state – albeit the much slower evolutionary one. Through the immediate pressures upon the individuals in a population, not only those individuals but also the whole population may change – by adaptive modification, or by poor adaptation and eventual decline and possible extinction. The last misfortune overcame the Labrador duck, a close relative of the eider, which became extinct something over a century ago, probably because it could not escape human predation by retreating northwards to breed. Adaptation to a changing environment is therefore necessary for any successful species. An eider comes into the world programmed, as it were, to show or develop certain responses to the important characteristics of its environment – including other eiders and any other animal that affects it significantly, particularly predators. But although the programming is quite detailed and exact, there is still enough plasticity in the eider population as a whole for adaptations to take place to changing conditions. As Charles Darwin pointed out in 1859 the individuals in a population are varied, and the struggle for existence is based upon these variations resulting in the survival of the fittest. The eider's range of geographical distribution – both latitudinal and longitudinal, its diversification into recognisably distinct subspecies, and its wide range of potential prey species (although it prefers molluscs) are all indications of a successful animal.

But what is success? It is reflected by all of the factors I have just mentioned, and also by the numbers of individuals of a species present in the total population. These all add up to express the degree of success of a species' adaptations to environment to date. But we must also take into account the potential of the animal to adapt to future change – its plasticity in the face of the necessity to adapt further. Highly specialised species of animals therefore run the risk of the environment changing in such a way that they cannot survive the change by adaptation. They have, as it were, put all their eggs in one basket. The eider has not done this. It is still generalised enough to be able to cope with any likely environmental changes other than deliberate attempts at extermination by man.

When it comes to comparing an animal like the eider with the human species the problems are enormous. And we are only just beginning to realise what the problems are, let alone work out ways of dealing with them. Not only is there the difficulty of making comparisons between man and the other animals because of the variety of ways in which genetically controlled adaptations show themselves, but also there is the problem that man is now subject to cultural evolution which, as far as we know, is not under genetical control except very indirectly. This cultural evolution involves the handing down of information and instructions concerning the human's adaptations to its environment from generation to generation by means of education, upbringing, and the media. Some other animals do show a primitive form of cultural evolution in that the young may learn from their parents how to deal with a particular environmental situation. For example, the young of those oystercatchers which specialise in feeding upon mussels learn, over a period of many months, a specific and quite complex method of opening these bivalve shells and dealing with the contents. But this is a very different situation from the human state in which a vast amount of complex information is passed on directly from adults to young, and in which – perhaps more significantly – the complexity of cultural transfer is increasing at a greatly accelerating rate year by year.

In the Canadian tundra I was impressed very strongly by the fact that the indigenous people of the same area – the Eskimos – wherever they had managed to maintain their cultural identity in the face of the seductions of the white man's "civilisation" were much more at one with their environment and with themselves than the outsiders who were trying to "civilise" them. Yet these Eskimos were far from primitive. True, they live very close to nature, in an almost constant battle with the elements, and by "sophisticated" human standards their lives leave very much to be desired; yet they seemed to be not only efficient and successful in their mode of life, but also happy and contented. The frustrations and malfunctions which bedevil contemporary human society as a whole were noticeably absent. And indications of an advanced human state, such as sense of humour and the aesthetic appreciation of art forms, were not hard to find.

I am by no means proposing a "return to nature" or supporting the "noble savage" attitude, but I feel there is a lesson to be learnt here. We have to admit that many of the problems now threatening the so-called civilised world can be regarded as behavioural malfunctions, and it is perhaps worth doing a bit of

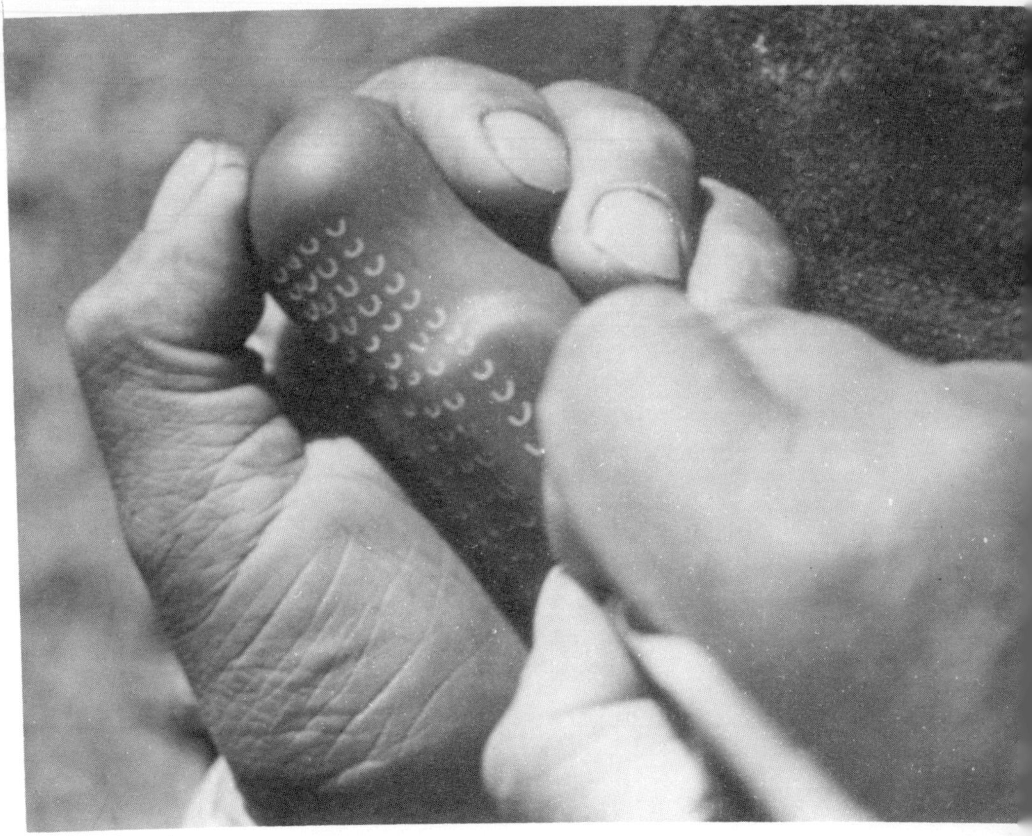

An eskimo carving the feather patterns on an owl

"naked apery" and looking at man as just another animal. A highly complex and advanced animal we are, to be sure, but one basically subject to similar pressures to those operating upon other species. It is often claimed that we are "conquering our environment" as a result of the enormous advances in technology we have achieved over the last few generations. Yet this achievement has brought with it an enormous increase in the stresses suffered by those who live in the technological society. As a result of the widespread ignorance of the basic biological processes which operate upon and within all animal species, including man, we are pushing one major aspect of our advanced abilities towards the limit, while ignoring the potential and actual effects this may have upon the individual and the community. The thalidomide tragedy is a case in point. But there are many other, less clear-cut, examples of communal malfunction which also suggest that we should stop and think; take a long, clear look at what we know about the nature of life; and try to decide what it is we should be doing and where we are going. For example, the educated biologist has known for many years that if you overcrowd a gregarious animal in a restricted environment that does not allow it to have access to the full range of environmental factors which it is "programmed" to interact with, then that animal becomes overstressed, highly malfunctional, and eventually stops breeding. Rats or mice in such restricted conditions, even if provided with ad lib food, water, and shelter, show both internal and external symptoms of excessive stress which are very similar to those shown by many people who live in high-rise apartment block conditions.

To take another example, it is clear that the survival of the more advanced animals – certainly the birds and mammals – depends partly upon what in human terms we would call "discipline" in the young. If an eider duckling of tender age does not come when it is called by the parent, or parent-substitute, then it may be in considerable danger from environmental perils. As a general rule the more complex an animal is, and the bigger it is when adult, and the longer lived it is, then the longer is the period of infancy and adolescence and the more important the activities of parental care. The human species is by far the most complex animal, and one of the largest and longest-lived. Also, the necessity for the handing down of cultural information from generation to generation greatly accentuates the importance of a well-organised upbringing so that the growing child is protected from environmental dangers and given the best opportunity for learning some of the basics of the complex human cultural system. On all counts one could be forgiven for assuming that the human young needs a more careful, disciplined, and well-organised upbringing than lower mammals, and birds such as the eider.

I must emphasise at this point that discipline does not mean restriction – except where necessary for guarding. But it does mean firm direction of attention in the young; otherwise how are they going to learn which of the vast array of environmental features of their world are the important ones which they have to learn how to interact with? To a skilled teacher the generation of enthusiasm for learning in the young is not difficult. But, sadly, it cannot be claimed that this faculty is possessed by many teachers; though it is not the individual's fault, but that of a diffused, confused, and biologically ignorant educational hierarchy. This blocking of enthusiasm in the young is particularly serious for our species for we possess an "exploratory drive" of a much more highly developed and longer-lasting form than any other animal. And it plays a very important part in the development of the child's mind. As Professor Niko Tinbergen has put it: "The conditions under which exploratory learning flourishes are security, a minimum amount of interference by adults (as distinct from guarding), time and opportunity, and an environment which invites exploration." I believe this to be a very important statement which we ignore at our peril.

I believe that undisciplined, unorientated, yet restrictive educational practices are responsible for much of the malaise in human children today. But of course this is only part of the story. Maternal deprivation also figures very significantly in the list of biological malfunctions present in our society today, the mothers themselves being overstressed and unable to perform their natural, evolved, maternal functions. When we also consider the increasing incident of the "battered baby" syndrome, to say nothing of inter-sexual strife, crime, drug-addiction, and suicide, the over-all picture is, in biological terms at least, a very grim one. We are beginning to come to terms with the problem of ecological pollution, that is, the pollution of our physical environment, but we have hardly begun to consider the problem of the pollution of inter-personal relationships: what I call "behavioural pollution".

If success necessarily involves continued plasticity and the ability to adapt to further environmental change – and from our studies of other organisms this would certainly appear to be so – it would seem that present-day man is less successful than he has been in the past. In Professor Tinbergen's words: " ...the behaviour student considers it very well possible, indeed likely that we are reaching a point where the 'viability gap' – the gap between what our new habitat requires us to do and what we are actually doing – is becoming so wide that our behavioural adjustability is already now being taxed to the limit. The conclusion seems inescapable that we shall soon be faced with a task of 'bio-engineering' for the purpose of restoring our adaptedness, or rather of re-establishing adaptedness at a new level . . . In this task we cannot possibly succeed unless we know *in concreto* the new pressures that we are creating, and how these pressures could be either met or reduced. And while functional ethology helps us in identifying these pressures, it will be the knowledge of behaviour mechanisms, and of mechanisms of behaviour development that will have to form the basis for whatever engineering will have to be undertaken."

In this book I have tried to give a picture of an ethologist at work and of the behaviour patterns which are revealed as a result of that work. I leave it to the reader to decide whether such an approach to behaviour in general and, ultimately, human behaviour in particular, is valid or not. Having worked with a wide variety of animals – eiders and humans being only two of them – over a period of more than a quarter of a century, I believe that much of our hopes for the future of man, and hence the other animals also, lies in the biology of behaviour. In the words of one of the greatest of all biologists, Thomas Henry Huxley: "Sit down before fact as a little child, be prepared to give up every preconceived notion, follow humbly wherever and to whatever abysses nature leads, or you shall learn nothing."

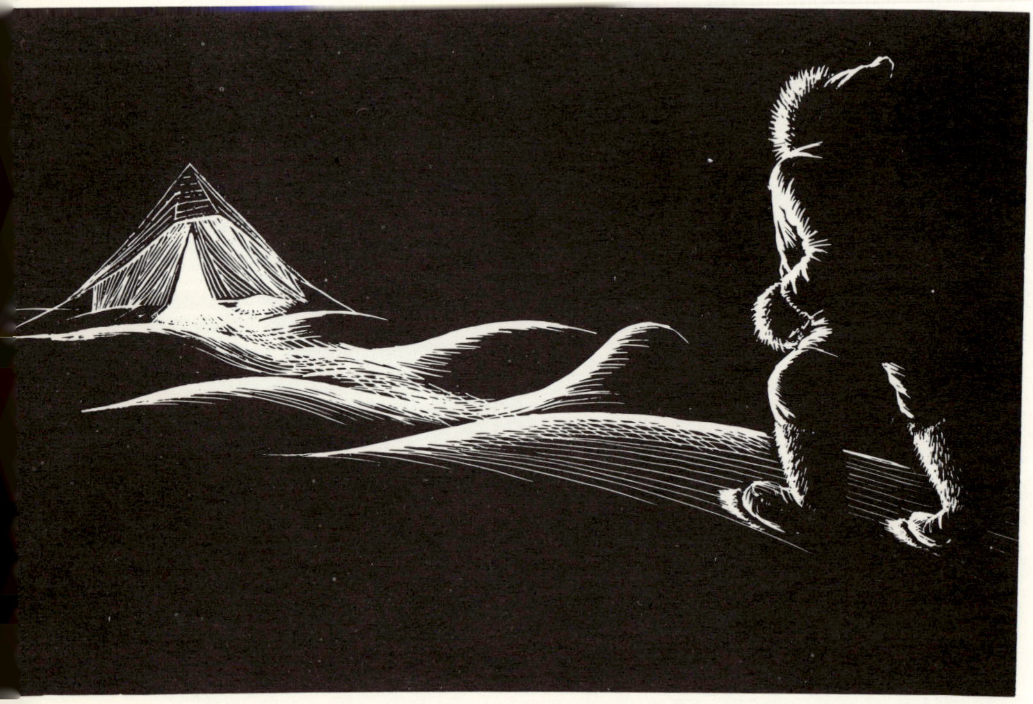

Appendices

Appendix 1
Works for Reference and Further Reading

This list must, of necessity, be highly selective, and I am therefore naming a few key works for the major areas of interest covered in this book. They are all authoritative and respected and many of them guide the reader to other works.

Anyone interested in the history of arctic exploration should read the two volume work by Fridtjof Nansen *In Northern Mists.* Long out of print, this can still be obtained second-hand or from libraries, and the author was himself, of course, one of the greatest of arctic explorers and scientists. For antarctic adventure and heroism one cannot do better than Apsley Cherry-Garrard's *The Worst Journey in the World.* This was undoubtedly the most difficult exploration ever undertaken in pursuit of ornithological knowledge. And for exploration across oceans *The Kon-Tiki Expedition* by Thor Heyerdahl, *Sailing Alone Around the World* by Joshua Slocum, or anything by Francis Chichester, are all excellent.

A general natural history list pertinent to the work described in this book could be enormous. No naturalist should be unacquainted with Gilbert White's *The Natural History of Selbourne,* probably the greatest natural history classic in the English language. For a contemporary view of the state of natural history study, Niko Tinbergen's *Curious Naturalists* is hard to beat. The same author's *Social Behaviour in Animals* is also very useful. Konrad Lorenz' *King Solomon's Ring* is a must.

For the more ornithological side of things James Fisher's *A History of Birds* is very good, and the best text book is probably *The Life of Birds* by J.C. Welty. *A New Dictionary of Birds* edited by A. Landsborough Thomson is definitive, and no ornithologist can ignore the five volume *Handbook of British Birds* by Witherby et al or the shorter *Popular Handbook of British Birds* edited by P.A.D. Hollom. Ornithology and travel are beautifully combined in *Wild America* by Roger Tory Peterson and James Fisher.

For evolution, Charles Darwin's *The Origin of Species* is in a class of its own. It has a strong claim to be one of the most important books ever written. The same author's *The Descent of Man,* and *The Expression of the Emotions* are also very important indeed. *The Theory of Evolution* by J. Maynard Smith provides a very good assessment of recent developments in the science.

The contemporary human state as seen from the biological viewpoint is out-lined in *The Naked Ape* by Desmond Morris. His books *The Human Zoo,* and *Intimate Behaviour* are also instructive. General surveys are also given in Robert Ardrey's *African Genesis, The Territorial Imperative,* and *The Social Contract.* A challenging synthesis of psychiatry and ethology is given in *Human Behaviour* by Claire and W.M.S. Russell. And two books by important scientists which excitingly reveal their attitude to their life and work are *The Inequality of Man* by J.B.S. Haldane, and *The Stress of Life* by Hans Selye. I hope some of the books I have mentioned will give the reader the excitement and satisfaction they have given me.

Appendix 2
Acoustic Signals of Eider Duckling

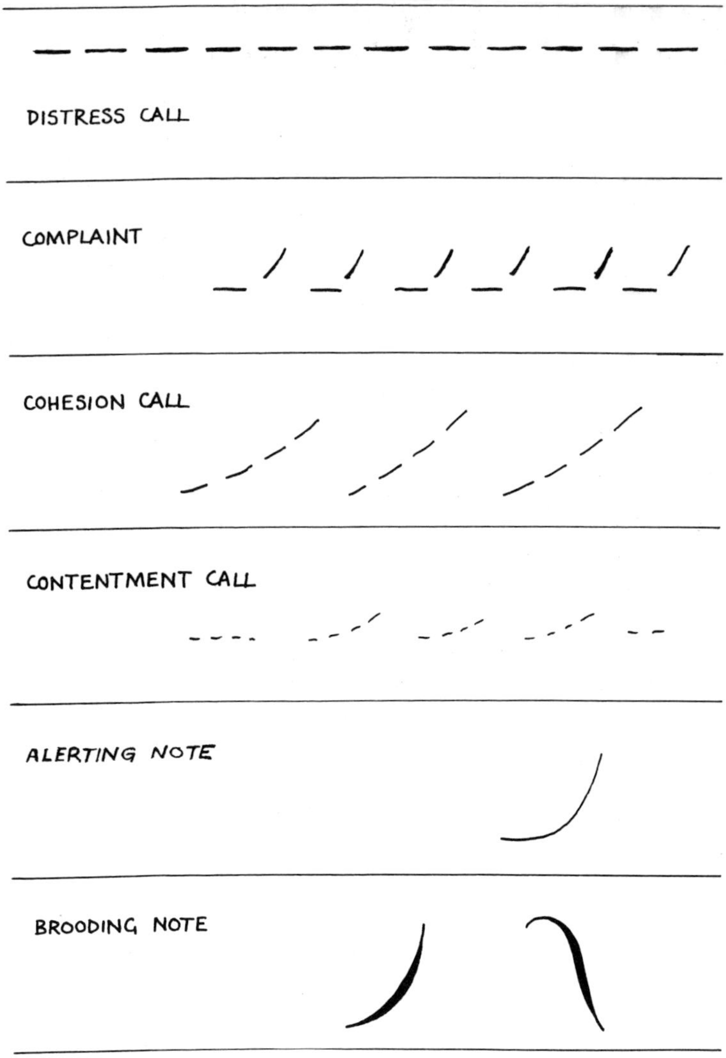

These drawings give a rough idea of the differences between the calls. Horizontally, length of line indicates length of call; vertically, height of line indicates pitch of call; and thickness of line indicates loudness of call. Thus the distress call is a loud, high-pitched repeated single note, while the cohesion call is a most subdued rising pattern of a few notes

Appendix 3
Organisation of Some Eider Duckling Instincts

It must be stated first of all that such diagrams (see opposite) are not meant to indicate physical connections between cause and effect, stimulus and response, but are models based upon observation which might help us to understand what goes on in the bird's tiny mind.

All the arrows in this diagram indicate connections or sequences which I have observed myself under natural conditions. But they are by no means the only connections possible, partly because of the limitations of drawing 4 dimensional processes in 2 dimensions, and partly because one's observations are always incomplete. For example, in the topmost connections water in the bill does not *always* result in drinking by means of the upward nod. It may result in bill-shaking to eject that water as occurs in preening wet plumage.

If we take the defence instinct rectangle however, we can see how observed connections between cause and effect may help us to understand how different inputs to the brain might be organised into different outputs to fixed action patterns. Sometimes, for example, a duckling's distress call may result in other ducklings distress calling; at other times, according to circumstances, it may result in the ducklings bunching in the female's danger shadow. These comments should help the reader to understand what this diagram is all about.

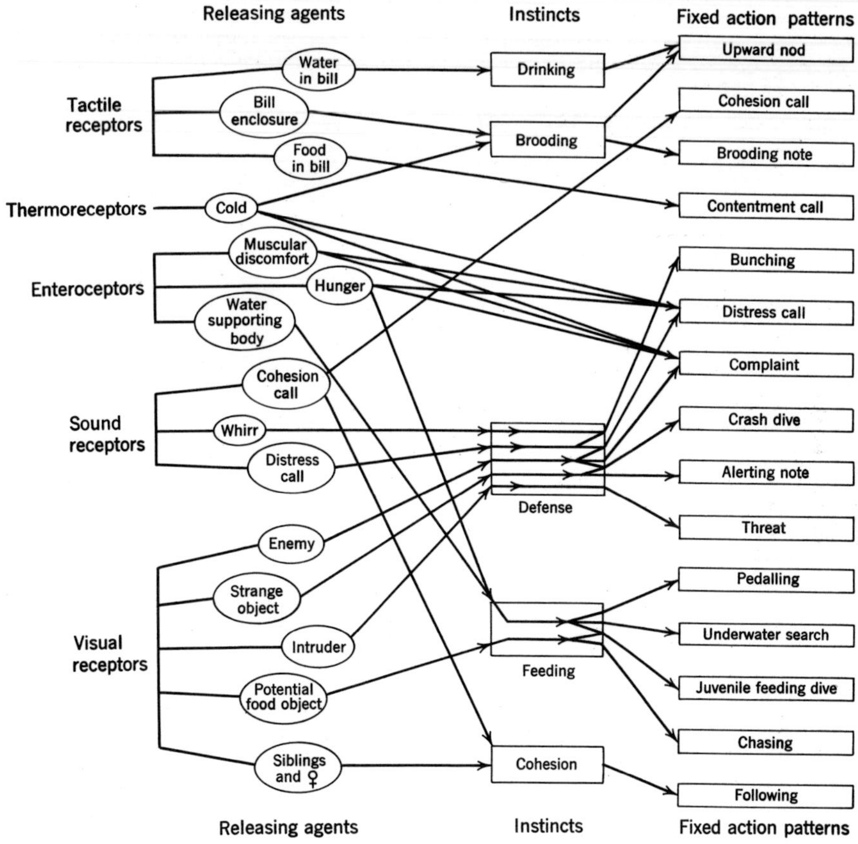
Releasing agents
Instincts
Fixed action patterns
Tactile receptors
Water in bill
Bill enclosure
Food in bill
Thermoreceptors
Cold
Enteroceptors
Muscular discomfort
Hunger
Water supporting body
Sound receptors
Cohesion call
Whirr
Distress call
Visual receptors
Enemy
Strange object
Intruder
Potential food object
Siblings and ♀
Drinking
Brooding
Defense
Feeding
Cohesion
Upward nod
Cohesion call
Brooding note
Contentment call
Bunching
Distress call
Complaint
Crash dive
Alerting note
Threat
Pedalling
Underwater search
Juvenile feeding dive
Chasing
Following
Releasing agents
Instincts
Fixed action patterns

Appendix 4
Basic Sequence of Movements in Juvenile Feeding Dive

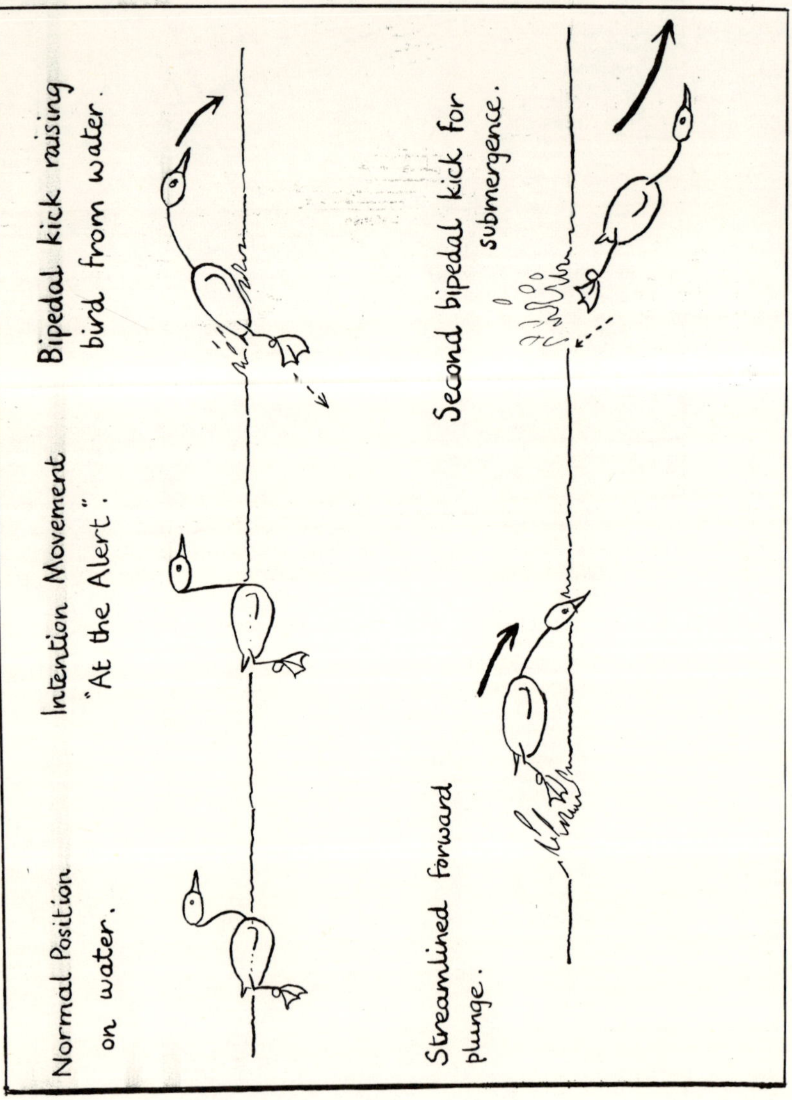

Index